MW00605143

Masters & their Pieces

best of furniture design

The Deutsche Nationalbibliothek lists this publication in
the Deutsche Nationalbibliografie; detailed bibliographical
data are available on the internet at http://dnb.d-nb.de.

ISBN 978-3-03768-097-1
© 2012 by Braun Publishing AG
www.braun-publishing.ch

The work is copyright protected. Any use outside of the
close boundaries of the copyright law, which has not
been granted permission by the publisher, is unauthor-
ized and liable for prosecution. This especially applies
to duplications, translations, microfilming, and any sav-
ing or processing in electronic systems.

2nd edition 2013

Editor, layout: Manuela Roth
Editorial staff: Anne Osherson
Translations (German): Cosima Talhouni
Art direction: Michaela Prinz, Berlin

All of the information in this volume has been compiled
to the best of the editor's knowledge. It is based on the
information provided to the publisher by the manufacturers and the designers' offices and excludes any li-
ability. The publisher assumes no responsibility for its
accuracy or completeness as well as copyright discrep-
ancies and refers to the specified sources (manufacturers and designers' offices). All rights to the photographs
are property of the photographer (please refer to the
picture credits).

Masters & their Pieces

Manuela Roth

best of furniture design

BRAUN

Foreword
Geleit

Dear readers,

Without a doubt a great many books have already been written about classic furniture design. Art historians have declared furniture a cultural artefact, and comprehensively presented it by style and epoch. Tribute has also been paid to furniture designers and architects in numerous exhibitions, publications and auctions. Yet which designs have been most widely embraced by our society over the last 100 years? Which masterpieces have found their way not only into our museums, but also into our homes?

This book looks at the 42 most important furniture designers and their greatest works. All of the pieces featured have one thing in common: they are still – or again – being produced. That was the principal criterion for inclusion. After all, why not let the market be the judge of good design? No company can afford to continue making products that don't sell. The selection featured in this book serves two purposes: it offers a retrospective look at furniture design and a current overview of the most important items still sold at selected furniture stores.

Perhaps it would have been fairer to the designers to have arranged them in alphabetical order. However, for the purposes of this book, it made more sense to follow the dates of birth of the designers. It is astonishing to see the design quality of Mies van der Rohe's work, all the more so when presented in the context of his time. We also see how long it took most designers to achieve a genuine breakthrough with their work. Thus, it comes as little surprise that one of the youngest designers included in the book, Stefan Diez, recently turned forty.

We hope you enjoy this trip into our world of furniture design.

Wilfried Lembert
Chairman of the Supervisory Board
Creative Inneneinrichter GmbH & Co.KG

Liebe Leserinnen, liebe Leser,

sicherlich wurden über Designer und Möbelklassiker schon viele Bücher geschrieben. Möbel wurden als Kulturgüter von Kunsthistorikern aufgearbeitet und in zeitlicher Ordnung dem Publikum präsentiert, Designer und Architekten nach Ausstellungen, Veröffentlichungen und Auktionsergebnissen gewürdigt. Wessen Entwürfe sind aber wirklich in den letzten 100 Jahren in einer breiteren Gruppe unserer Gesellschaft angekommen? Wessen Meisterstücke haben nicht nur den Weg in unsere Museen, sondern auch in unsere Wohnungen gefunden?

Das vorliegende Buch beschäftigt sich mit den 42 wichtigsten Möbeldesignern und deren besten Entwürfen. Alle Möbelobjekte haben eines gemein, sie sind immer noch – oder wieder – in Produktion. Das ist die Vorgabe für die Auswahl der Produkte. Ist nicht auch der Markterfolg ein Gradmesser für gute Gestaltung? Kein Unternehmen kann es sich leisten, nicht kommerziell erfolgreiche Produkte weiter herzustellen. Das Buch schafft durch diese Auswahl zweierlei, eine Retrospektive des Möbeldesigns und eine aktuelle Übersicht der wesentlichen Einrichtungsgegenstände, die heute immer noch in ausgewählten Einrichtungshäusern erwerbbar sind.

Um allen Gestaltern gleichermaßen gerecht zu werden, hätte man sicherlich eine alphabetische Reihenfolge wählen können. Sinnvoller ist der vorliegende Aufbau des Buches nach dem Geburtsjahr der Designer. Man ist überrascht, welche unglaubliche Gestaltungsqualität die Entwürfe Mies van der Rohes aufweisen, vor allem wenn man sie im Kontext zur damaligen Zeit betrachtet. Man stellt aber auch gleichermaßen fest, wie lange es dauert, bis ein Designer den wirklichen Durchbruch schafft. So ist es vielleicht auch nicht verwunderlich, dass einer der Jüngsten im Buch, Stefan Diez, gerade seinen vierzigsten Geburtstag gefeiert hat.

Viel Spaß beim Eintauchen in unsere Welt,

Wilfried Lembert
Vorsitzender des Aufsichtsrats
Creative Inneneinrichter GmbH & Co.KG

Content
Inhalt

006	Preface		
007	Vorwort		
008	Eileen Gray	142	Alberto Meda
014	Ludwig Mies van der Rohe	148	Lievore, Altherr, Molina
020	Le Corbusier	158	Antonio Citterio
030	Alvar Aalto	168	Ron Arad
036	Mart Stam	174	Fernando & Humberto Campana
040	Marcel Breuer	182	Rodolfo Dordoni
044	Jean Prouvé	192	Naoto Fukasawa
050	Arne Jacobsen	202	Piero Lissoni
060	Egon Eiermann	216	Maarten van Severen
068	Charles & Ray Eames	220	James Irvine
078	Eero Saarinen	226	Axel Kufus
082	Hans J. Wegner	232	Jasper Morrison
090	Harry Bertoia	242	Patricia Urquiola
094	Achille Castiglioni	258	Hella Jongerius
100	Fritz Haller & Paul Schärer	262	Werner Aisslinger
104	Verner Panton	268	Konstantin Grcic
108	Pierre Paulin	278	Jean-Marie Massaud
116	Poul Kjærholm	290	EOOS
124	Dieter Rams	302	Philipp Mainzer
130	Mario Bellini	310	Ronan & Erwan Bouroullec
136	Toshiyuki Kita	318	Stefan Diez

timelessly beautiful

What makes a piece of furniture a masterpiece, and which pieces retain their appeal, even after decades? Design is certainly a key factor; quality design endures, continuing to exert a fascination even after many years. Those designs perceived as fresh and exciting by successive generations convey a particular idea that never loses its relevance. A classic piece may represent the spirit of its age, but should never be fashionable. A timeless, essential form must not only be aesthetically appealing, but more importantly must remain true to its function. Good design involves not only form but also the right choice of materials and colors.

Which classic items of furniture are suitable for daily use, and which can find a place in our homes and lives even today? Nobody wants to live in a museum, and so the first requirement of furniture is utility; it must be durable, easy to care for and functional.

This book presents furniture designs from the last 100 years that have what it takes to be called design classics. These are not stylised objets d'art, but rather impress us by their enduring functionality. They can easily be part of our daily life, as all of them are still being produced. The spectrum extends from the understated tubular steel furniture of the 1920s to the kooky plastic furniture and organic forms of the 1960s, right through to the present day.

The 42 master designers featured in this volume are arranged in chronological order. In this way, their work is placed within its proper context. This approach also allows the reader to spot interesting points of contact between the different designers. For example, the fact that Marcel Breuer and Mart Stam experimented together with tubular steel at the Bauhaus. Also, that Charles & Ray Eames and Eero Saarinen were close friends from their college days and worked together. This book clearly shows that the leading designers of the last century were often years ahead of their time. Many of the designs that are so highly valued today were not mass-produced until several years after their creation.

This book also illustrates the development of furniture design over the last century. Thanks to new materials and production techniques, we are still seeing the creation of furniture that is both revolutionary and timeless. For example, the 'Waver' chair by Konstantin Grcic draws on materials from the world of outdoor sports to create a kind of modern hammock. Stefan Diez, meanwhile, employs materials and technology from the automobile industry to create his 'Chassis' chair, using lightweight space-frame technology.

Masters & their Pieces – best of furniture design presents the milestones in the history of furniture and its master designers. Embark on a journey into the world of modern furniture design, from the timeless classics to the masterpieces of tomorrow.

Zeitlos schön

Was macht ein Möbelstück zum Klassiker, welche Möbel verlieren auch nach Jahrzehnten nichts von ihrer Anziehungskraft? Ein entscheidendes Kriterium ist sicherlich das Design, denn gutes Design ist dauerhaft und übt auch nach vielen Jahren noch eine Faszination aus. Ein Entwurf wirkt dauerhaft frisch und begeistert auch noch nachfolgende Generationen, weil er eine Idee vermittelt, die immer aktuell ist. Ein Klassiker darf den Zeitgeist repräsentieren, aber nicht modisch sein. Eine zeitlose Form, auf das Wesentliche reduziert, muss nicht nur ästhetisch sein, sondern vor allem ihrer Funktion gerecht werden. Zum guten Design gehört neben der Form auch die Auswahl der passenden Materialien und Farben.

Und welche Klassiker sind alltagstauglich, und können auch heute in unsere Wohnung und in unser Leben integriert werden? Niemand wohnt gerne wie in einem Museum, Möbel müssen also den Anforderungen an den Alltag gerecht werden und müssen langlebig, pflegeleicht und vor allem funktional sein.

Im vorliegenden Buch werden Möbelentwürfe der letzten 100 Jahre bis heute präsentiert, die das Zeug zum Klassiker haben. Sie werden nicht als Kunstobjekte stilisiert, sondern überzeugen vor allem im täglichen Gebrauch. Sie lassen sich problemlos in unseren Alltag integrieren, denn alle werden heute noch produziert. Die Bandbreite reicht von den reduzierten Stahlrohrmöbeln der 1920er Jahre, über poppige Kunststoffmöbel und organische Formen der 1960er, bis in die aktuelle Zeit.

Die vorgestellten 42 Meister-Designer sind chronologisch geordnet. So werden ihre Entwürfe in den zeitlichen Kontext gestellt und lassen interessante Verbindungen der Designer untereinander erkennen. So haben zum Beispiel Marcel Breuer und Mart Stam gemeinsam am Bauhaus an neuartigen Stahlrohrmöbeln experimentiert. Auch Charles & Ray Eames und Eero Saarinen verband eine enge Freundschaft, die aus ihrer gemeinsamen Studentenzeit her rührt und auch zu gemeinsamen Arbeiten geführt hat. Es wird deutlich, dass die führenden

Köpfe des letzten Jahrhunderts ihrer Zeit oft viele Jahre voraus waren. Viele der heute so geschätzten Stücke sind erst einige Jahre nach ihrer Entstehungszeit in die Massenproduktion gegangen.

Auch die Entwicklung der Möbel der letzten 100 Jahre wird illustriert. Dank neuer Materialien und neuartiger Produktionstechniken werden auch heute noch Möbel entwickelt, die revolutionär und zeitlos schön sind. Der Stuhl „Waver" von Konstantin Grcic zum Beispiel greift auf moderne Materialien aus dem Outdoor-Sportbereich zurück um eine Art moderne „Hängematte" zu kreieren. Für den Stuhl „Chassis" griff Stefan Diez auf Materialien und Technologie aus der Automobilindustrie zurück: das Gestell wird in leichtgewichtiger Space-Frame-Technologie produziert.

Masters & their Pieces – best of furniture design präsentiert die Meilensteine in der Geschichte der Möbel und ihre Meister. Erleben Sie eine Zeitreise durch das moderne Möbeldesign, von den zeitlosen Klassikern bis zu den Meisterwerken von morgen.

The Day Bed is accessible from all sides, and looks equally inviting and comfortable from any perspective, allowing it to be placed freely in a room.

Das Day Bed ist von allen Seiten zugänglich und sieht aus allen Blickwinkeln immer einladend und komfortabel aus, sodass es frei im Raum platziert werden kann.

all images: manufacturer ClassiCon, authorized by The World Licence Holder Aram Designs, Ltd. London

Eileen
Gray

Eileen Gray (August 9, 1878 – October 31, 1976) was an Irish furniture designer and architect. Although she remained somewhat obscure during her career, she is now regarded as a leading figure in 20th century architecture and design, with considerable impact in both the Modernist and Art Deco movements.

In 1898, Gray enrolled in the Slade School of Fine Art, where she studied painting, then went on to continue her studies in Paris. In 1906, she started working for Seizo Sugawara, a master of lacquer work. After World War I, Gray was commissioned to decorate an apartment, for which she designed furniture, carpets and lamps, as well as custom lacquered panels for the walls, all to much acclaim. Gray's success allowed her to open up a small shop in Paris. Although influenced by the same ideals as her contemporaries Le Corbusier and Charlotte Perriand, her style was generally a more opulent and lavish take on Modernism. She incorporated the tubular steel structures into her chair designs, like the imposing "Bibendum" chair, but hers were luxuriously upholstered in leather. Much of her interior design continued to prominently feature her lacquer work. 1937, she agreed to exhibit her design for a holiday center in Le Corbusier's Esprit Nouveau pavilion at the Paris Exposition, but World War II soon put an end to her career. Although she worked on a few projects after the war, she became more and more reclusive, and was largely forgotten until the late 20th century.

Eileen Gray (9.8.1878–31.10.1976) war eine irische Innenarchitektin und Designerin. Obwohl sie während ihrer Karriere recht unbekannt blieb, wird sie doch heute als eine der führenden Architektinnen und Designerinnen des 20. Jahrhunderts, die einen entscheidenden Einfluss auf den Modernismus und Jugendstil-Bewegungen hatten, betrachtet.

1898 begann Gray ihr Studium der Malerei an der Slade School of Fine Art in London und studierte danach in Paris. 1906 begann sie für Seizo Sugawara zu arbeiten, einem Meister der Lackkunst. Nach dem Ersten Weltkrieg wurde Gray beauftragt eine Wohnung zu dekorieren. Sie entwarf hierfür Möbel, Teppiche, Lampen sowie maßgefertigte Lackpaneele für die Wände; alles Arbeiten, die große Anerkennung fanden. Basierend auf diesem Erfolg konnte Gray ein kleines Geschäft in Paris eröffnen. Obwohl sie die gleichen Ideale wie ihre Zeitgenossen Le Corbusier und Charlotte Perriand verfolgte, war ihr Stil eine allgemein etwas opulenter und aufwändiger inszenierte Interpretation des Modernismus. Ihre Stühle, z.B. der Stuhl „Bibendum", enthielten die Stahlstangenkonstruktionen ihrer Zeit, aber mit luxuriöser Lederpolsterung. Der größte Teil ihrer Innenarchitekturentwürfe enthielt weiterhin ihre Lackarbeiten. 1937 genehmigte sie die Ausstellung ihres Entwurfes für ein Freizeitzentrum in Le Corbusiers Esprit Nouveau Pavillon in der Weltausstellung von Paris.

Der Zweite Weltkrieg beendete ihre Karriere. Obwohl sie an einigen Projekten nach dem Krieg arbeitete, zog sie sich zunehmend zurück und geriet bis Ende des 20. Jahrhunderts größtenteils in Vergessenheit.

The Monte Carlo sofa's expansive curves and clever use of empty space make it a remarkable icon of 20th century design.

Die ausladenden Kurven des Sofas Monte Carlo zusammen mit der geschickten Nutzung leeren Raumes machen es zu einem absoluten Kultobjekt des 20. Jahrhunderts.

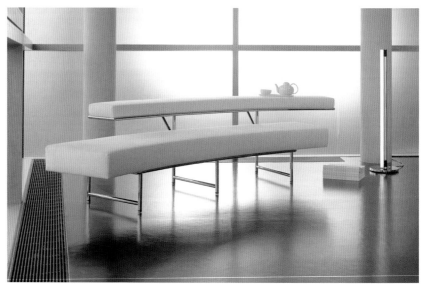

The Jean table was created for the E 1027 summer villa, which Gray designed with Jean Badovici. Every room in the house was furnished with one of these steel and wood tables.

Der Tisch Jean wurde für die Sommervilla E 1027 entwickelt, die Gray zusammen mit Jean Badovici entwarf. Jeder Raum im Haus enthielt einen dieser Tische aus Stahl und Holz.

The strict and simple line of the steel Tube Lamp, shown here with the Bibendum chair, speaks of Gray's design moving from Art Déco Functionalism.

Die strengen und einfachen Linien der Stahllampe Tube, im Bild zusammen mit dem Stuhl Bibendum, zeigt den Übergang Grays Designstil vom Jugendstil zum Funktionalismus.

The Lota sofa was designed for Madame Mathieu-Levy's apartment on Rue de Lota in Paris, an eloquent example of French interior architecture of the 1920s. Featuring luxuriant cushions and lacquered sidepieces.

Das Sofa Lota wurde für die Wohnung der Madame Mathieu-Levy in der Rue de Lota in Paris entworfen. Es ist ein ausdrucksvolles Beispiel französischer Innenarchitektur der 1920er Jahre mit luxuriösen Kissen und lackierten Seitenteilen.

The Wendingen rug was a tribute to a Dutch journal of architecture that first presented Gray's work. The rug is now widely considered to be a masterpiece of textile design.

Der Teppich Wendingen war ein Dankeschön an eine holländische Architekturzeitschrift die als erste Grays Designs vorstellte. Der Teppich wird heute allgemein als ein Meisterstück des Textildesigns angesehen.

The iconic Barcelona® Chair was created for the 1929 Barcelona International Exposition. The ornate leather seat, made of individual squares welted together, is supported by a brilliant, curved metal frame.

Der legendäre Stuhl Barcelona® wurde für die Weltausstellung in Barcelona 1929 entworfen. Der Ledersitz aus einzelnen, zusammengefügten Quadraten wird von einem glänzenden, gebogenen Metallrahmen gestützt.

Barcelona® is a registered trademark of Knoll, Inc.

Ludwig
Mies van der Rohe

Ludwig Mies van der Rohe (March 27, 1886 – August 17, 1969) was a German architect, and a pioneer of Modern architecture. His clarity of design and use of modern materials such as steel and glass defined early 20th century German design. Mies's first professional experience was working for his father, a master stonemason, followed by an apprenticeship with furniture designer Bruno Paul in Berlin. He then joined the architecture office of Peter Behrens, whose work is widely regarded as a precursor of the modern movement, before establishing his own office in Berlin in 1912. He was soon commissioned to build a number of upper-class homes, which he created using simple volumes reminiscent of the Prussian Neo-Classical style of the early 19th century. In the early 1930s, Mies became the last director of the Bauhaus design school, but was soon forced to close it under pressure from the Nazi Party. In 1938, he emigrated to Chicago. He designed the campus of the Illinois Institute of Architecture, where he later became director of architecture.

Mies's approach to furniture design was similar to his approach to architecture. He employed the newest industrial technologies available to create furniture in the modern styles. Many of his pieces, like the "Barcelona® chair" and the "Brno chair", whose leather upholstery and chrome frames create an engaging contrast between traditional luxury and sleek modernity, have become icons of modernist design.

Ludwig Mies van der Rohe (27.3.1886–17.8.1969) war deutscher Architekt und ein Vorreiter der Moderne. Die Klarheit seiner Entwürfe und die Verwendung moderner Materialien wie Stahl und Glas waren richtungsweisend für deutsches Design Anfang des 20. Jahrhunderts.

Mies sammelte erste professionelle Erfahrungen im Unternehmen seines Vaters, einem Steinmetzmeister. Nach einer Zeit bei dem Möbeldesigner Bruno Paul in Berlin arbeitete er im Architekturbüro von Peter Behrens, dessen Arbeiten als die Vorläufer der Moderne betrachtet werden. 1912 eröffnete Mies sein eigenes Büro in Berlin, wo er bald eine Reihe von Häusern für wohlhabende Bauherren mit schlichten Volumen entwarf, die an den preußischen Klassizismus-Stil des frühen 19. Jahrhunderts erinnerten. Anfang der 1930er Jahre wurde Mies der letzte Direktor des Bauhauses in Dessau, das aber bald darauf unter dem Druck der nationalsozialistischen Partei geschlossen wurde. 1938 siedelte er nach Chicago über, wo er den Campus des Illinois Institute of Architecture entwarf und wo er später die Leitung der Architekturabteilung übernahm.

Auch im Möbelbau wandte er neueste Technologien an um modernste Möbel zu entwerfen. Viele seiner Arbeiten, wie der „Barcelona®" Sessel und der Stuhl „Brno", dessen Lederpolsterung und Chromrahmen einen ansprechenden Kontrast zwischen traditionellem Luxus und modernem Chic bilden, sind Kultobjekte modernistischen Designs geworden.

The Barcelona® Collection also includes a daybed.
The polished wood frame rests on four tubular
steel legs, and 72 individual squares of leather
are used in the upholstery.

Zu der Barcelona® Kollektion gehört auch ein
Daybed. Der polierte Holzrahmen sitzt auf vier
Stahlrohrbeinen, während 72 einzelne Leder-
quadrate für das Polster verwendet wurden.

The S 533 R Chair is a cantilever chair whose
steel base is a long, sweeping curve, and is more
elongated than most other cantilever designs. The
seat itself is made of lightweight wicker.

*Der Stuhl S 533 R Chair ist ein Freischwinger
dessen Stahlbasis wie eine langgezogene Wölbung
geformt ist die länglicher als die meisten anderen
freischwingenden Designs ist. Der Sitz selbst ist
aus leichtem Korbmaterial hergestellt.*

The seamless cantilever frame of the Brno Chair is available in either tubular steel or flat bar steel, and the simplicity of the design was created to complement a house Mies had designed in Brno.

Der nahtlose, freischwingende Rahmen des Stuhls Brno Chair besteht entweder aus Metallrohr oder Flachstahl. Sein schlichtes Design wurde für ein Haus entwickelt welches Mies in Brno entworfen hatte.

The Krefeld Lounge Chair was also designed with a specific house, in this case, two German villas, in mind. The simple, elegant chair is made of hardwood and upholstered in fabric or leather.

Der Klubsessel Krefeld wurde auch für ein spezifisches Haus entwickelt, diesmal zwei deutsche Villen. Der einfache elegante Sessel ist aus Hartholz hergestellt und mit Stoff oder Leder bezogen.

The Four Seasons Bar Stool was designed for the Four Seasons Hotel in New York City. The cantilever frame is reduced to its most basic form: with no backrest or armrests, one simple curve remains.

Der Barhocker Four Seasons wurde für das Four Seasons Hotel in New York City entworfen. Der freischwingende Rahmen ist auf seine einfachste Form reduziert: ohne Rücken- und Armlehnen bleibt nur eine einfache Wölbung erhalten.

*One of Le Corbusier's most recognizable designs,
LC-1 Sling chair uses the chrome-plated, tubular
steel frame to suspend the seat in mid-air. The
seat can be tilted as the sitter shifts positions.*

*Eines von Le Corbusiers bekanntesten Designs,
der Stuhl LC-1, hat einen verchromten Stahlrohrrahmen, der die Sitzfläche frei schweben lässt.
Die Sitzfläche neigt sich, wenn der Benutzer seine
Position ändert.*

Le Corbusier

Charles-Édouard Jeanneret, better known as Le Corbusier (October 6, 1887 – August 27, 1965), a Swiss-born French architect, designer, writer, and painter, was one of the most influential figures in 20th century design and urban planning. He studied architecture in Switzerland, Vienna, and Berlin, and like many thinkers of the early 20th century, Le Corbusier soon became interested in urbanism. He believed that better design leads to an overall better quality of life, and his early work was aimed at improving the living conditions of residents of crowded cities. He approached urban planning by designing what he called "machines for living": functional, high-rise residential blocks, which could provide quality homes at low cost. The Unité d'Habitation in Marseilles, built in 1952, included shops, a gym, and even a rooftop swimming pool. These early housing projects were the blueprints for much of urban planning today.

Until the late 1920s, he had been relying on mass produced furniture to furnish his architectural projects, but after the architect Charlotte Perriand joined his studio, they started to experiment with creating their own pieces. The first of these were tubular steel chairs with chrome plating, which were exhibited in Paris in 1929 as part of his collection for the Salon d'Automne. The most famous of his furniture designs, however, are undoubtedly the elegant chairs, stools, and sofas of the "LC series".

Charles-Édouard Jeanneret, besser bekannt als Le Corbusier (6.10.1887–27.8.1965), war ein französischer Architekt, Designer, Schriftsteller und Maler schweizerischer Herkunft. Er war eine der einflussreichsten Persönlichkeiten des Design und der Städteplanung des 20. Jahrhunderts.

Er studierte Architektur in der Schweiz, in Wien und Berlin und interessierte sich für den Urbanismus. Da er der Überzeugung war, dass besseres Design zu einer allgemein besseren Lebensqualität führe, zielten seine frühen Arbeiten auf die Verbesserung der Lebensumstände der Bewohner überfüllter Städte. Sein städtebaulicher Ansatz waren die von ihm entworfenen „Wohnmaschinen": funktionelle Hochhäuser, die hochwertigen Wohnraum zu niedrigen Kosten boten. Zu der Unité d'Habitation in Marseilles, 1952 gebaut, gehörten Läden, eine Sporthalle und sogar ein Swimming Pool auf dem Dach. Heutige städtebauliche Maßnahmen basieren zu großem Teil auf diesen frühen Wohnprojekten.

Bis Ende der 1920er Jahre verwendete er in seinen architektonischen Projekten serienmäßig produzierte Möbel, aber nachdem die Architektin Charlotte Perriand zu seinem Büro hinzustieß, fingen sie gemeinsam an mit der Herstellung eigener Stücke zu experimentieren. Die ersten Möbel waren verchromte Stahlrohrstühle, die 1929 in Paris als Teil der Sammlung für den Salon d'Automne ausgestellt wurden. Le Corbusiers berühmteste Möbel sind aber die eleganten Stühle, Hocker und Sofas der „LC Serie".

The LC-2 sofa and armchair were called the "cushion baskets." The frame is externalized, but instead of being the focus of the piece, it discreetly braces heavy leather upholstery.

Das Sofa und der Sessel LC-2 wurden die „Kissenkörbe" genannt. Der Rahmen ist von außen ersichtlich, aber statt im Fokus des Designs zu stehen, stützt er nur diskret die schweren Lederpolster.

The glass tabletop of the LC-10-P table is anchored to the ground by wide steel legs, creating a striking visual contrast between the fragile surface and its industrial supports.

Die gläserne Tischplatte des Tisches LC-10-P ist mit ausladenden Stahlbeinen im Boden verankert. Dies ergibt einen auffälligen optischen Kontrast zwischen der zerbrechlichen Oberfläche und ihren industriellen Stützen.

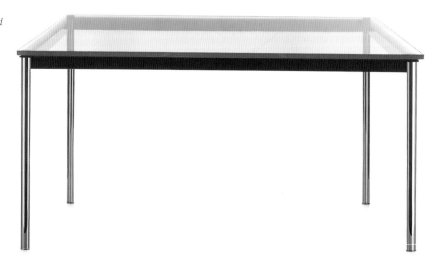

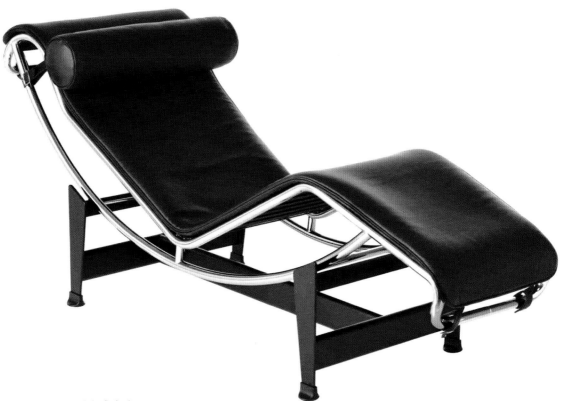

The LC-4 lounge chair, nicknamed the "relaxing machine," floats above its steel frame. Its curves mirror the natural curves of the body, and the simple leather upholstery preserves its clear lines.

Der Liege LC-4 mit dem Spitznamen „Entspannungsmaschine" schwebt über seinem Stahlrahmen. Ihre Kurven folgen der natürlichen Anatomie des Körpers, während die schlichte Lederpolsterung ihre klaren Linien hervorhebt.

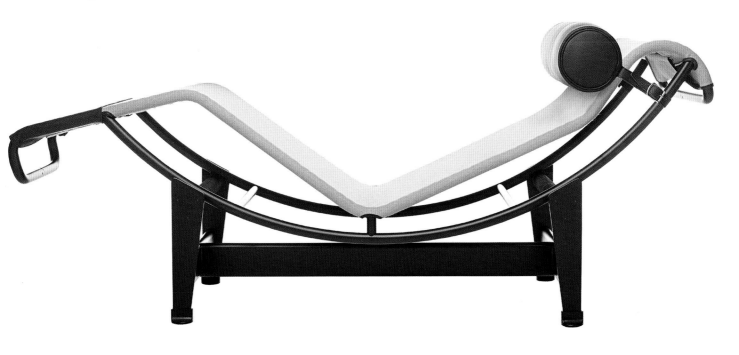

The LC-3 armchair and sofa differ from the LC-2 only in the choice of upholstery. The more compact LC-2 is upholstered in leather, while down cushions gives the LC-3 a softer look and feel.

Sofa und Sessel LC-3 unterscheiden sich nur in ihrem Bezug von der Serie LC-2. Die kompakteren LC-2 - Möbel haben Lederbezüge, während Daunenkissen der Reihe LC-3 eine weichere Optik und Haptik geben.

The LC-14 stool was first designed for a university residence in Paris. Made of chestnut wood instead of le Corbusier's usual steel, the holes carved into the sides make it easy to move around.

Der Hocker LC-14 wurde ursprünglich für eine Universitätswohnung in Paris entwickelt. Er ist – im Gegensatz zu dem von Le Corbusier am häufigsten verwendeten Material Stahl – aus Kastanienholz gefertigt. Durch die Löcher in den Seiten ist er einfach zu transportieren.

The LC-3 series was later revised to produce a second, weather-resistant version. The original stainless steel frame remains, but the upholstery is lined with canvas or polyester.

Die Serie LC-3 wurde später überarbeitet, um eine zweite, wetterfeste Variante zu produzieren. Der ursprüngliche Edelstahlrahmen wurde übernommen, die Polster aber sind mit Segeltuch oder Polyester bezogen.

The LC-7 Swivel Chair was designed for designed for the Modern Art Salon in Paris in 1929. The chrome-plated tubular steel frame curves sharply downwards, and the seat above swivels freely.

Der Drehstuhl LC-7 wurde 1929 für den Modern Art Salon von Paris entworfen. Der verchromte Stahlrohrrahmen ist stark nach unten abgewinkelt und der Sitz darüber frei drehbar.

The revolving stool LC-8 was an exploration of the structural possibilities that would be available when using tubular steel. It was designed to mirror the LC7 swivel chair.

Der Drehhocker LC-8 war das Resultat einer Unter-suchung der strukturellen Möglichkeiten die sich durch die Nutzung von Stahlrohr ergeben. Er wur-de als Replikation des Drehstuhls LC7 entworfen.

The LC-15 Table combines a round, wood tabletop with sharp steel angles in the base, for a play on geometrical forms as well as materials.

Der Tisch LC-15 ist die Kombination einer runden Holztischplatte mit Stahlwinkeln als Untergestell. Das Ergebnis ist ein Spiel aus geometrischen Formen und Materialien.

The Tokyo Chaise-Longue was conceived by
Charlotte Perriand while she was living in Japan.
She re-created the LC-4 using bamboo, "giving the
"relaxing machine" an new, organic feel".

Die Tokyo Chaise-Longue wurde von Charlotte
Perriand während ihrer Zeit in Japan entworfen.
Sie bildete den LC-4 aus Bambus nach, was der
„Entspannungsmaschine" eine neue, organische
Note gab.

Another design which Perriand conceived in Japan, the Ombra Lounge Chair adds a distinctive lacquered finish to the steel frame. The slender frame supports two detachable leather cushions.

Ebenfalls von Perriand in Japan entworfen, fügt der Klubsessel Ombra eine einzigartige Lackierung zu dem Stahlrahmen hinzu. Der schlanke Rahmen stützt zwei abnehmbare Lederkissen.

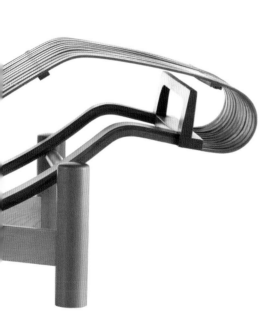

The 400 armchair's dramatic bent wood frame, low-slung seat and substantial upholstery have earned it the nickname "the tank."

Die hängende Position des Sitzes und die breiten Armlehnen des Stuhls 400 brachten ihm den Spitznamen „Tank Chair" ein.

Alvar
Aalto

Alvar Aalto (February 3, 1898 in Kuortane – May 11, 1976 in Helsinki) also known as "the Father of Modernism", was a Finnish architect and designer. Aalto's career, which lasted from the 1920s to the 1970s, was influenced by the Nordic Classicism that dominated the early 20th century, and by the International Style Modernism during the 1930s, but by the 1940s, he had developed his own, distinct Modernist style. Throughout his entire career, his approach to design can be characterized by the idea of Gesamtkunstwerk, or total work of art. He would design the building itself, then the interior surfaces and finally design the lighting, the furniture, and even the glassware.

Aalto's furniture designs often centered around wood, and he invented his own process for bending and shaping wood, which seemed to test the very limits of the material. The most well-known example of this process is the natural birch "Chair 69", which features the clean, organic lines that became Aalto's trademark. Another famous project of his was the Paimio Sanatorium, completed in 1932, for which he designed the "Paimio Armchair". Thanks to his bent wood technique, the armchair's backrest was specifically angled to help tuberculosis patients breathe more easily. Aalto's innovative use of wood greatly influenced other designers, including Charles and Ray Eames and Eero Saarinen.

Alvar Aalto (3.2.1898 in Kuortane – 11.5.1976 in Helsinki), auch als „Vater der Moderne" bekannt, war ein finnischer Architekt und Designer.

Aaltos Karriere, welche von den zwanziger bis in die siebziger Jahre des letzten Jahrhunderts reichte, war sowohl von dem nordischen Klassizismus beeinflusst, der am Anfang des 20. Jahrhunderts bestimmend war, als auch von dem internationalen Modernismus der dreißiger Jahre. In den 1940er Jahren allerdings entwickelte er seinen eigenen, unverwechselbaren modernistischen Stil. Während seiner ganzen Karriere verfolgte er den Gedanken des Gesamtkunstwerks. Er entwarf zunächst das Gebäude selbst, dann die Innenflächen und zuletzt die Beleuchtung, die Möbel und sogar das Geschirr. Aaltos Möbelentwürfe basierten oft auf Holz und er entwickelte seine eigene Methode für das Biegen und Formen von Holz, die bis an die Belastungsgrenzen des Materials ging. Das bekannteste Beispiel dieser Methode ist der „Chair 69" aus natürlichem Birkenholz, welcher die sauberen organischen Linien vorweist, die Aaltos Markenzeichen sind. Ein weiteres bekanntes Projekt war das Paimio Sanatorium, welches im Jahr 1932 fertig gestellt wurde und wofür er den Sessel „Paimio" entwarf. Dank seiner Holzformungs-Methode wurde der Rücken des Sessels in einem spezifischen Winkel, der Tuberkulose-Patienten half besser zu atmen, gebeugt.

Aaltos innovative Verwendung von Holz inspirierte andere Designer, wie zum Beispiel Charles und Ray Eames und Eero Saarinen.

Chair 41, the Paimio armchair, takes bent
plywood to an almost sculptural level. The seat is
formed by a single, thin sheet of wood that rolls
up under itself like a scroll.

Chair 41, der Sessel Paimio, ist mit gebogenem
Sperrholz so kunstfertig gestaltet, dass fast der
Eindruck einer Skulptur entsteht. Die Sitzfläche
besteht aus einer einzigen dünnen Holzplatte, die
in sich selbst wie eine Schriftrolle gebogen ist.

Chair 69 is made of bent birch wood, and the simple design allows the natural beauty of the material to shine.

Das schlichte Design des Stuhls 69 aus gebogenem Birkenholz unterstreicht die natürliche Ausstrahlung des Materials.

The E60 stool's distinctive L-shaped legs make it easily recognizable as well as stackable.

Die markanten L-förmigen Beine des Hockers E60 machen ihn leicht erkennbar; außerdem ist er gut stapelbar.

Aalto's tea trolley's lightweight wooden frame is paired with eye-catching, oversized wheels, making it as functional as it is whimsical.

Aaltos Teewagen kombiniert einen leichten Holzrahmen mit auffälligen überdimensionalen Rädern, was ihn praktisch und gleichzeitig skurril erscheinen lässt.

Armchair 406's cantilevered frame is upholstered with linen webbing, making it particularly lightweight and airy.

Der freitragende Rahmen des Sessels 406 ist mit geflochtenen Leinenstreifen umhüllt, was ihn besonders leicht und luftig macht.

The inspiration for the Aalto vase's wavy design has never been revealed. The serene shape has been surrounded in mystique since its debut 1937, and it has been an international sensation ever since.

Aalto hat nie verraten, was ihn zu der gebogenen Aalto-Vase inspiriert hat. Seit diese im Jahr 1937 vorgestellt wurde, ist die ruhige Form von einem geheimnisvollen Nimbus umgeben und wurde zu einer internationalen Sensation.

Daybed 710 is a versatile piece. The signature birch frame is topped with a lightweight mattress, and is easily converted from a sofa into a sleeping unit.

Daybed 710 ist ein vielseitiges Möbelstück. Es besteht aus einem Birkenholzrahmen, der zu Aaltos Markenkennzeichen wurde, ist bedeckt von einer leichten Matratze und sehr einfach von einem Sofa zu einem Schlafplatz verwandelbar.

The S33 chair, created in 1927, was a collaboration with Marcel Breuer. Together, the two designers experimented with flexible steel tubing to create furniture for the Stuttgart Weißenhofsiedlung.

Aus einer Zusammenarbeit mit Marcel Breuer für die Stuttgarter Weißenhofsiedlung und Experimenten mit biegsamem Stahlrohr ging 1927 der S33 hervor.

Mart
Stam

Mart Stam (August 5, 1899 – February 21, 1986) was a Dutch architect, urban planner, and furniture designer. His career spanned several decades, and therefore several important periods in design history, but his pragmatic, functional style generally falls into the New Objectivity movement.

Stam's first professional experience was as a draftsman in an architecture firm. In 1922, he was selected to design urban infrastructure plans for The Hague region, then he moved to Berlin, and was soon designing buildings across Germany. He first developed his cantilever chair in 1926, using parts of gas pipes and pipe joint fittings to create a tubular steel frame. He is widely credited as being the first to design this kind of chair, which has no legs in the traditional sense, and is supported instead by a curved metal frame. This iconic chair almost immediately started a whole new genre of chair design: similar models were created by Ludwig Mies van der Rohe, Eileen Gray, and Marcel Breuer. In 1930, Mart Stam was one of 20 architects who were commissioned by the Soviet Union to create new, Stalinist cities. He returned the Netherlands in 1934, where he began an academic career with the position of director at the Institute of Industrial Arts. This led to a professorship at the Academy of Figurative Arts in Dresden in 1948, and then to becoming a director at the Advanced Institute of Berlin in 1950. He retired in 1966, moving to Switzerland and withdrawing from public life.

Mart Stam (5.8.1899–21.2.1986) war ein niederländischer Architekt, Stadtplaner und Möbeldesigner. Seine Karriere erstreckte sich über mehrere Jahrzehnte und reichte deshalb auch über mehrere wichtige historische Epochen, obwohl sein pragmatischer, funktioneller Stil am ehesten der Neuen Sachlichkeit zuzuordnen ist.

Seinen beruflichen Werdegang begann Stam als technischer Zeichner in einem Architekturbüro. 1922 wurde er ausgewählt, neue Infrastrukturpläne für die Region um Den Haag zu entwickeln. Er zog daraufhin nach Berlin, von wo er bald Gebäude in ganz Deutschland plante. Im Jahr 1926 entwickelte er auch seinen berühmten freischwingenden Stuhl, der keine Beine im traditionellen Sinne aufweist, sondern stattdessen ein Traggestell aus verchromtem Stahlrohr. Dieser Stuhl mit Kultsymbolcharakter war schnell der Auslöser für eine ganze Gattung von Designerstühlen, denn ähnliche Modelle finden sich auch bei Ludwig Mies van der Rohe, Eileen Gray und Marcel Breuer. 1930 war Mart Stam einer von 20 Architekten, die von der Sowjetunion beauftragt wurden neue stalinistische Städte zu entwerfen. Er kehrte 1934 in die Niederlande zurück, wo er eine akademische Karriere als Direktor des Institutes für industrielle Kunst und später als Professor in Dresden (1948) und in Berlin (1950) antrat. Er setzte sich 1966 zur Ruhe und ließ sich in der Schweiz nieder, wo er sich aus dem öffentlichen Leben zurückzog.

The S34 chair includes armrests. Instead of simply adding them on top of the original chair, the frame itself was reformed so that the upper curve becomes armrests, while the seat is suspended below.

Stuhl S34 hat Armlehnen. Anstatt diese nur einfach an den ursprünglichen Stuhl anzubringen, wurde der Rahmen selbst so umgeformt dass die obere Wölbung zu Armlehnen wurde, während der Sitz darunter hängt.

The S43 chair went into series production in 1931, as an optimized version of the S33. The clear, restrained form is a stunning example of Modernist design.

Der S43 ging 1931 in Serienproduktion, als optimierte Variante des S33. Die klare, zurückhaltende Form macht ihn zu einem beispielhaften Entwurf für den Geist der Moderne.

S32 is Breuer's original cantilever chair, designed
in 1927. The continuous, tubular steel frame is
carefully engineered to be perfectly supportive
even without traditional back legs.

S32 ist der ursprüngliche Freischwinger von
Breuer, 1927 entworfen. Der durchgängige Stahlrohrrahmen ist genauestens konstruiert, um auch
ohne traditionelle Stuhlhinterbeine optimalen Halt
zu bieten.

Marcel
Breuer

Marcel Breuer (May 21 1902, in Pécs, Hungary – July 1, 1981 in New York City) was a Hungarian-born architect and furniture designer of the Modernist movement, whose modular construction and simple forms earned him much acclaim over the course of his career.

He studied at the Bauhaus school of design, where he later became a teacher and the head of the school's carpentry program. His early designs made extensive use of steel, especially tubular steel frames. Breuer's earliest prototype of a tubular steel chair dates back to 1925, and he claimed to have been inspired by the handlebars of his bicycle. Later in his career, Breuer returned to his roots as a carpenter, producing a range of experimental furniture made of bent and curved plywood. Breuer fled Germany after the rise of the Nazi party and settled in the United States, where he taught at the Harvard School of Architecture and designed several houses with his colleague Walter Gropius. One such project was the Alan I W Frank House in Pittsburgh, which they designed as a "total work of art," creating the furniture and interior design as well as the building itself. In 1953, Breuer was commissioned to design the UNESCO headquarters in Europe, which marked the beginning of a new direction in his career. Working primarily with concrete, and designing much larger projects, like the Whitney Museum of American Art in New York City, Breuer became one of the pioneers of Brutalism, a highly geometric movement that followed Modernism.

Marcel Breuer (21.5.1902, in Pécs, Ungarn – 1.7.1981 in New York City) war ein Architekt und Möbeldesigner der Moderne ungarischer Herkunft, der für seine modulare Bauweise und schlichten Formen berühmt war.

Er studierte am Bauhaus, wo er später selbst unterrichtete und die Tischlereiabteilung leitete.

Für seine frühen Arbeiten benutzte er ausgiebig Stahl, vor allem Stahlrohrrahmen. Breuer sagte von seinem ersten Prototyp eines Stahlrohrstuhles aus dem Jahr 1925, dass er von dem Lenkrad seines Fahrrades inspiriert worden sei. Im weiteren Verlauf seiner Karriere kehrte Breuer zu seinem Ursprung als Tischler zurück und entwarf eine Reihe von Versuchsmöbeln aus gebogenem Schichtholz. Breuer floh aus Deutschland während des Naziregimes und ließ sich in den USA nieder, wo er an der Harvard School of Architecture unterrichtete und verschiedene Häuser zusammen mit seinem Kollegen Walter Gropius entwarf. Eines dieser Projekte war das Alan I W Frank-Haus in Pittsburgh, welches inklusive den Möbeln und der Innenausstattung als „Gesamtkunstwerk" entworfen wurde. 1953 wurde Breuer beauftragt, das UNESCO Hauptquartier in Europa zu entwerfen, was seiner Karriere eine neue Wendung gab. Indem er hauptsächlich mit Beton arbeitete und viel größere Projekte wie das Whitney Museum of American Art in New York City entwarf, wurde Breuer einer der Vorreiter des Brutalismus, einer sehr geometrischen Bewegung, die auf den Modernismus folgte.

In the S285 desk, wooden surfaces seem to float on a tubular steel frame. In true Bauhaus style, function and aesthetic are seamlessly combined to create clear and elegant design.

Beim Schreibtisch S285 scheinen Holzoberflächen auf einem Stahlrohrrahmen zu schweben. In echtem Bauhaus-Stil sind Funktionalität und Ästhetik nahtlos kombiniert, um ein klares und elegantes Design zu erzielen.

Breuer continued his experiments with tubular steel frames with the B22 side piece, which he created during his time at Bauhaus. B22 can be used as a table or as a shelf.

Mit B22, welches er in seiner Bauhauszeit entwarf, setzte Breuer seine Experimente mit Stahlrohrrahmen fort. B 22 kann als Tisch oder Regal genutzt werden.

The B9 stacking side tables, which can be easily moved around and stored, were originally used in the cafeteria of Walter Gropius's Bauhaus building.

Die stapelbaren Beistelltische B9, welche einfach umgestellt und gelagert werden können, wurden in der Cafeteria des Bauhaus-Gebäudes von Walter Gropius verwendet.

The Standard Chair is a work of logic and practicality. The back legs are heavier because they take most of the weight, but strict functionality is tempered with a dynamic and versatile aesthetic.

Der Standard Chair ist das Resultat von Logik und Zweckmäßigkeit. Die hinteren Beine sind schwerer da sie das meiste Gewicht tragen, aber die pure Sachlichkeit ist durch eine dynamische und vielseitige Ästhetik veredelt.

Jean
Prouvé

Jean Prouvé (April 8, 1901 – March 23, 1984) was a French metal worker, designer, and architect of the early modernist movement. Prouvé is widely appreciated for introducing industrial manufacturing techniques, and an industrial aesthetic to interior design. He initially trained to be a blacksmith, then attended engineering school in his native Nancy. In 1923 he opened a workshop, where he produced wrought iron lamps, chandeliers, and other household objects. He soon expanded his range to include metal furniture of his own design. Throughout his career, Prouvé displayed more interest in the materials and in the production process than in form alone, and considered himself more of an engineer than a designer. His goal was to create unpretentious, materially efficient products. The "Standard" chair and the

"Antony" chair, created in 1934 and 1954, respectively, are prime examples of his modern, constructionally sound designs. His training as an engineer is most evident in the series of tables which he developed using his own innovative method of folding sheet metal. In the mid 1950s, Prouvé moved away from furniture design in favor of architecture, especially pre-fabricated housing. An auto-didact, he was very successful in this area as well, and his prototype of a pre-fabricated house is considered a major innovation in the field.

Jean Prouvé (8.4.1901–23.3.1984) war ein französischer Kunstschmied, Designer und Architekt des frühen Modernismus. Prouvé gelangte zu hohem Ansehen dadurch, dass er Produktionstechniken aus der Industrie und eine industrielle Ästhetik auf die Innenarchitektur übertrug.

Nach Abschluss einer Lehre als Kunstschmied besuchte er die Ingenieurschule in seiner Heimatstadt Nancy. 1923 eröffnete er seine eigene Werkstatt, wo er schmiedeeiserne Lampen, Leuchter und andere Haushaltsartikel herstellte. Bald erweiterte er sein Produktangebot um Möbelstücke, die er selbst entwarf. In seinen Arbeiten zeigte Prouvé mehr Interesse an den Materialien und an dem Herstellungsprozess als an der Form als solche und sah sich selbst mehr als Ingenieur denn als Designer. Sein Ziel war immer die Herstellung von schlichten, effizienten Produkten. Die Stühle „Standard" (1934) und „Antony" (1954) sind grundlegende Beispiele seines modernen, produktionstechnisch einwandfreien Designs. Sein Ingenieurshintergrund trat am deutlichsten zutage in der Tischserie, bei der er seine eigene innovative Methode für gefaltetes Walzblech anwendete. Mitte der 1950er Jahre entwarf Prouvé weniger Möbel, sondern konzentrierte sich mehr auf die Architektur, vor allen Dingen auf Fertighäuser. Als Autodidakt war er auch in diesem Bereich sehr erfolgreich und sein Prototyp eines Fertighauses wird als bahnbrechende Innovation betrachtet.

The Standard Chair (1934) combines wood and metal, which was revolutionary at the time. The seat and backrest are made of oak, while the frame is made of steel.

Der Standard-Chair (1934) kombiniert Holz und Metall, was zur damaligen Zeit revolutionär war. Sitz und Rückenlehne sind aus Eichenholz gefertigt, und die Beine sind aus Stahl.

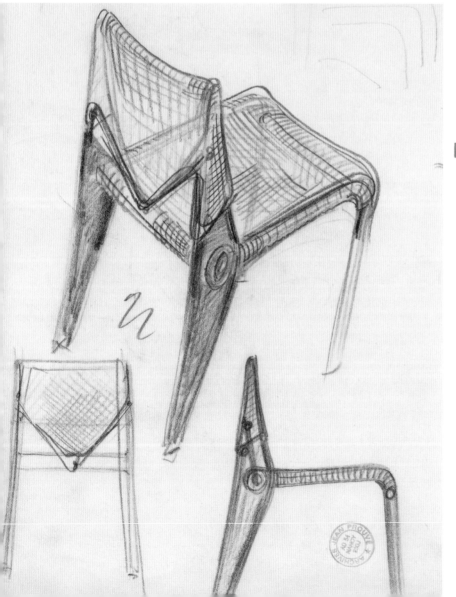

The Guéridon Table's clarity of form makes it a 20th century classic and a fine example of Prouvé's engineer approach to design. Only two shapes are used – a round top and three identical legs.

Die klare Formsprache des Tisches Guéridon macht ihn zu einem Klassiker des 20. Jahrhunderts und ist ein gutes Beispiel von Prouvés Ingenieuransatz in seinen Designs. Er benutz nur zwei Formen – eine runde Tischplatte und drei identische Beine.

Developed for one of Prouvé's early pre-fabricated housing projects, the EM Table's slanted legs are the same shape as those of the Guéridon, but this time in a four-legged design.

Entwickelt für eines von Prouvés frühen Fertighausprojekten, sind die abgeschrägten Beine des Tisches EM genauso geformt wie die des Guéridon, aber diesmal mit vier Beinen.

The Tabouret Haut, which simply means "high stool," mixes steel and wood for a sleek, modern design. The steel ring stabilizes the four long wooden legs, and complements the round seat.

Der Tabouret Haut, was einfach „hoher Hocker" bedeutet, kombiniert Stahl und Holz in einem eleganten modernen Design. Der Stahlring stützt die vier langen Beine und ergänzt den runden Sitz.

The Cité Lounge Chair, which was designed for the residence halls of Nancy's Cité Universitaire, is suspended between two wide steel frames. Leather armstraps soften the chair's industrial aesthetic.

Der Armlehnstuhl Cité Lounge Chair, ursprünglich für die Studentenwohnheime der Cité Universitaire in Nancy entwickelt, hängt zwischen zwei breiten Stahlrahmen. Armlehnen aus Lederstreifen mildern die industrielle Ästhetik des Stuhls.

The sturdy steel frame of the Antony chair supports a slender, high-backed wooden seat shell. The dynamic curves are echoed in both components, and tubular steel legs anchor the piece.

Der robuste Stahlrahmen des Stuhls Antony stützt eine schlanke hölzerne Sitzschale mit hohem Rücken. Die dynamischen Kurven sind in beiden Komponenten reflektiert, während Stahlrohrbeine das Möbel verankern.

Recently, the clothing company G-STAR launched Prouvé RAW, a limited-edition collection that re-imagines some of Prouvé's designs using new colors and materials.

Vor kurzem führte die Modefirma G-STAR die Prouvé RAW Kollektion ein. Diese limitierte Auflage lässt manche von Prouvés Designs wieder mit neuen Farben und Materialien aufleben.

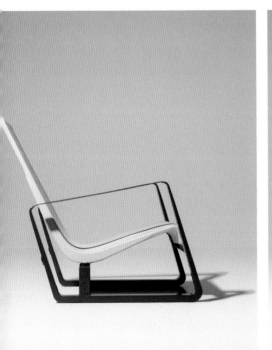

Series 7, designed in 1955, is by far the most sold
chair in the history of the collaboration between
Jacobsen and Fritz Hansen's. The four-legged,
stackable chair represents the culmination of the
lamination technique.

Series 7, 1955 entworfen, ist der bei weitem
meistverkaufte Stuhl in der Geschichte der
Zusammenarbeit von Jacobsen und Fritz Hansen.
Der vierbeinige stapelbare Stuhl ist der Höhepunkt
ihrer Laminationsmethode.

Arne
Jacobsen

Arne Jacobsen, (February 11,1902 – March 24, 1971) was a Danish architect and designer who contributed extensively to both the Danish Modern style and to architectural functionalism. Jacobsen studied architecture at the Royal Danish Academy of Fine Arts in Copenhagen, and won a silver medal in chair design at the Paris Art Deco Fair in 1925, before he even graduated. His early work drew inspiration from Le Corbusier as well as Ludwig Mies van der Rohe, but he soon developed his own, recognizable style. In 1930, he set up his own architectural office, and approached his first few projects with an all-encompassing attention to detail. When he was commissioned to design a seaside resort on the Danish coast, he created everything from the building to the uniforms of the employees, the tickets, and seasonal passes. In 1934, Jacobsen first started his collaboration with the Fritz Hansen furniture house, and their first major success was the "Ant" chair, in 1952. In 1955, "Series 7" enjoyed similar acclaim, cementing Jacobsen's status in the furniture world. At the end of the 1950s, he designed the Royal Hotel in Copenhagen, for which he developed three more of his most famous chairs and sofas – the "Egg", the "Swan", and "Series 3300". Today, Jacobsen's elegant furniture is still regarded as a great part of Danish cultural heritage.

Arne Jacobsen, (11.2.1902–24.3.1971) war ein dänischer Architekt und Designer, der viel zum dänischen Modernen Stil sowie zum architektonischen Funktionalismus beigetragen hat. Jacobsen studierte Architektur an der Königlich Dänischen Kunstakademie in Kopenhagen, und gewann 1925, schon bevor er sein Studium beendet hatte, eine Silbermedaille für Stuhl-Design von der Paris Art Deco Messe.

Seine frühen Arbeiten waren von Le Corbusier und Ludwig Mies van der Rohe inspiriert, aber er einwickelte bald seinen eigenen, unverkennbaren Stil. Im Jahre 1930 gründete er sein eigenes Architekturbüro und ging gleich seine ersten Projekte mit einer umfassenden Liebe zum Detail an. Als er beauftragt wurde, einen Badeort an der dänischen Küste zu entwerfen, lieferte er einen umfassenden Entwurf von den Gebäuden bis hin zu den Uniformen der Angestellten und den Tickets und Saisonausweisen. 1934 begann Jacobsen seine Zusammenarbeit mit dem Fritz Hansen Möbelhaus, dessen erster großer Erfolg der Stuhl „Ameise" im Jahr 1952 war. Die 1955 entworfene Stuhl-Serie „7" wurde ebenso bekannt und festigte Jacobsens Status als Möbeldesigner. Ende der 1950er Jahre entwarf er das Royal Hotel in Kopenhagen, für das er drei weitere seiner berühmten Stühle entwarf – das „Ei", den „Schwan", und die „Serie 3300".

Heute werden Jacobsens elegante Möbel noch immer als ein wichtiger Teil des dänischen Kulturgutes angesehen.

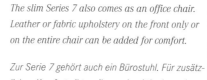

The slim Series 7 also comes as an office chair.
Leather or fabric upholstery on the front only or
on the entire chair can be added for comfort.

Zur Serie 7 gehört auch ein Bürostuhl. Für zusätzlichen Komfort gibt es ihn auch mit Leder- oder
Stoffpolsterung nur auf der Vorderseite oder über
den ganzen Stuhl.

Designed in 1952 for use in the canteen of the Danish pharmaceutical firm Novo Nordisk, the Ant Chair ("Myren" in Danish) was named for its ant-like silhouette.

1952 für die Kantine des Dänischen Pharmaunternehmens Novo Nordisk entworfen, wurde der Ameisenstuhl („Myren" auf Dänisch) nach seiner Ameisen-ähnlichen Silhouette benannt.

The lightweight, stackable Grand Prix dining
chair didn't just win the most prestigious award at
the Milan Trienniale – it was named for it.

Der leichte, stapelbare Esszimmerstuhl Grand
Prix gewann nicht nur den angesehensten Preis
der Triennale di Milano – er wurde auch nach ihm
benannt.

The Egg chair was originally designed for the lobby and reception areas of the Royal Hotel, in Copenhagen. Its sculptural shape guarantees a bit of privacy in public spaces.

Der Sessel Egg wurde ursprünglich für die Lobby und den Empfangsbereich des Royal Hotel in Kopenhagen entworfen. Seine skulpturale Form garantiert ein gewisses Maß an Privatsphäre in öffentlichen Bereichen.

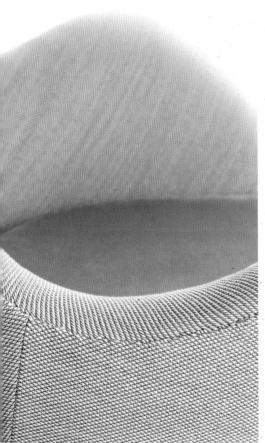

The Swan Sofa is all round lines and soft forms. The seat is upholstered in cashmere or leather and sits on an aluminum frame.

Das Sofa Swan besteht gänzlich aus runden Linien und weichen Formen. Der Sitz ist mit Kaschmir oder Leder gepolstert und sitzt auf einem Aluminiumrahmen.

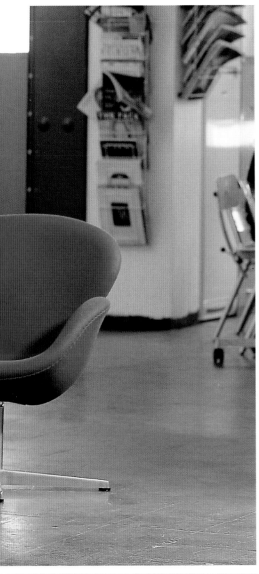

The Swan was also designed for the Royal Hotel in Copenhagen. The chair's swivel base allows guests to spin in their seat and become active participants in the busy hotel atmosphere.

Der Swan wurde auch für des Royal Hotel in Kopenhagen entworfen. Das drehbare Unterge-stell ermöglicht es Gästen sich auf ihren Sitzen zu drehen und so aktiv am Hotelgeschehen teilzunehmen.

The Oxford chair was originally designed for the professors at St. Catherine's College in Oxford. The chair's extra tall back served as a symbol of prestige and created a space of its own.

Der Stuhl Oxford wurde ursprünglich für die Professoren des St. Catherine's College in Oxford entworfen. Der extralange Rücken des Stuhls wurde zum Prestigesymbol.

The 3300 series consists of the one-seater easy
chair as well as the two-seater and three-seater
sofas.

*Die Serie 3300 besteht aus einem Sessel, einem
Zweisitzer, sowie einem Dreisitzer Sofa.*

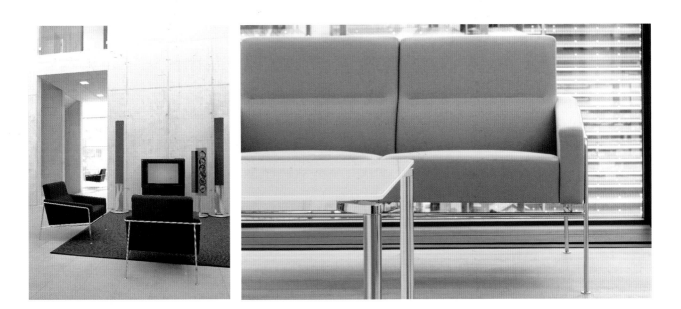

Combining a thin, steel frame with curved
plywood shells for the seat and backrest, the
minimalist SE 68 chair is one of Eiermann's most
famous design. The flexible materials provide
optimal comfort.

Mit seiner Kombination aus dünnem Stahlrahmen
und gebogenen Schichtholzschalen für die Sitzfläche und die Rückenlehne ist der minimalistische
Stuhl SE 68 eines von Eiermanns berühmtesten
Designs. Die flexiblen Materialien bieten Komfort
der Extraklasse.

Egon Eiermann

Egon Eiermann (September 29, 1904, Neuendorf – July 20, 1970, Baden-Baden) was a renowned German architect of the post-war period.

After studying at the Technical University of Berlin, he worked for a short time at the Karstadt Building department and was a partner in an architecture firm, before becoming a faculty member at the Technical University of Karlsruhe, where he developed steel frame construction methods. Eiermann embraced Functionalism, and some of his most famous works of architecture include a building for the German Parliament in Bonn and the new Kaiser Wilhelm Memorial Church in Berlin.

Eiermann also enjoyed much success and recognition as a furniture designer. After World War II, he was the first German designer to produce serialized furniture that met and surpassed the international standards for form and functionality. He is often credited as being the driving force that brought the German design world out of its dark years under National Socialism. He helped restore its connections to its illustrious past, like the legacy of Bauhaus, and was one of the leaders of Second Modernism. His designs are characterized by their clear, simple geometry, and their easily recognizable functions. In 1953, he designed his iconic desk, the "Eiermann Table Frame". "Eiermann Table Frame 2" was a modified version designed in 1965, which was lightweight and collapsible.

Eiermann co-founded the German Design Council in 1951, and received a number of prestigious awards during his lifetime, including Germany's Grand Order of Merit.

Egon Eiermann (29.9.1904 in Neuendorf – 20.7.1970 in Baden-Baden) war ein bekannter deutscher Architekt der Nachkriegszeit. Nach dem Architekturstudium an der Technischen Hochschule Berlin arbeitete er in dem Baubüro der Rudolph Karstadt AG in Hamburg und als Partner eines Architekturbüros, bevor er eine Stelle als Professor an der Technischen Hochschule Karlsruhe antrat.

Eiermanns Stil war der Funktionalismus; er war einer der führenden Architekten der zweiten Moderne. Das Abgeordneten-Hochhaus des Bundestags in Bonn sowie die neue Kaiser-Wilhelm-Gedächtniskirche in Berlin wurden von ihm entworfen.

Eiermann war auch als Möbeldesigner erfolgreich. Nach dem Zweiten Weltkrieg war er der erste deutsche Designer, der Möbel entwarf, die den internationalen Normen für Form und Funktion entsprachen und diese sogar übertrafen. Er wird oft als die treibende Kraft bezeichnet, die die deutsche Designerwelt aus den dunklen Jahren des Nationalsozialismus herausführte und die Verbindung zur Vergangenheit wieder herstellte, wie z.B. zur Bauhaus-Bewegung. Seine Entwürfe haben eine klare und einfache Geometrie und leicht erkennbare Funktionalität. 1953 entwarf er seinen legendären Schreibtisch, das Tischgestell „Eiermann 1". Das Tischgestell „Eiermann 2" war ein leichteres und zerlegbares Modell aus dem Jahre 1965.

Eiermann war Mitbegründer des Deutschen Rates für Formgebung im Jahre 1951 und erhielt viele hochrangige Auszeichnungen, wie z.B. den Verdienstorden der Bundesrepublik Deutschland.

SE 68 is a versatile piece that is equally suited to
schools, offices, libraries, or home settings.

SE 68 ist ein vielseitiges Möbelstück, das gleich
gut in Schulen, Büros, Bibliotheken und Wohn-
räume passt.

The SE 18 folding chair is made entirely out of
beech: the frame, with its tapered legs, is made
out of solid wood, and the seat and backrest are
made out of beech plywood.

*Der Klappstuhl SE 18 ist komplett aus Birke ge-
fertigt: Der Rahmen mit den verjüngenden Beinen
besteht aus Massivholz , während der Sitz und
Rücken aus Birken-Schichtholz gefertigt sind.*

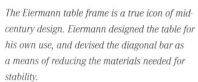

The Eiermann table frame is a true icon of mid-century design. Eiermann designed the table for his own use, and devised the diagonal bar as a means of reducing the materials needed for stability.

Der Eiermann Tischrahmen ist ein echtes Design-Kultobjekt der Mitte des letzten Jahrhunderts. Eiermann entwarf den Tisch für den Eigengebrauch und entwickelte die diagonale Stange um das Stützmaterial zu verringern.

The Children's Desk starts with the same design
as the original table frame, but both the table and
the accompanying chair are height-adjustable, so
that they can grow up along with the child.

*Der Kinderschreibtisch basiert auf dem gleichen
Design wie der ursprüngliche Tischrahmen, aber
der Tisch und der passende Stuhl sind höhenver-
stellbar sodass sie mit dem Kind wachsen können.*

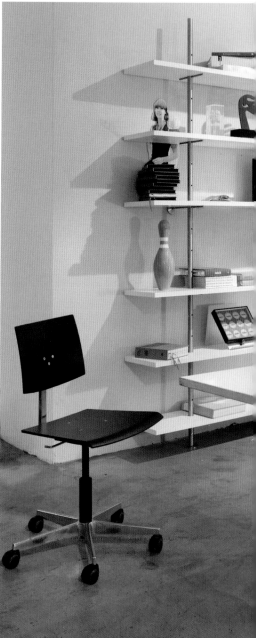

Eiermann's Shelving System was the prototype for what is a very common shelving solution today. Since it is mounted on a wall, the shelving system needs very little additional materials for structure.

Eiermanns Regalsystem war der Prototyp für eine heutzutage sehr verbreitete Regallösung. Da es an der Wand befestigt wird, braucht das System sehr wenig zusätzliches strukturelles Material.

Stool 38 comes either as a standard stool or a higher bar stool, the latter of which has a supportive metal ring around the legs. Like the SE 68, the frame is made of steel while the seat is wooden.

Den Hocker 38 gibt es entweder als Standard-Hocker oder als einen höheren Barhocker. Dieser hat einen stützenden Metallring um seine Beine. Wie der SE 68, ist sein Rahmen aus Stahl und der Sitz aus Holz.

The Plastic Armchair with dowel-leg base has a simple form sculpted to cradle the body, a deep, flexible seat, rounded edges for comfort, and stylish wooden dowel legs.

Der Plastic Armchair mit Rundholz-Beinen hat eine schlichte Form die den Körper umhüllt, eine tiefe flexible Sitzfläche, sowie gerundete Kanten und elegante Rundhölzer als Beine.

Manufacturing and distribution of Eames furniture designs and the Eames Trademark are the exclusive property of Herman Miller, Inc and Vitra.

Charles & Ray
Eames

Charles Eames (1907–1978) and Bernice "Ray" Eames (1912–1988) were an American design team who made tremendous contributions to contemporary architecture and furniture design. Married in 1941, they collaborated on an extensive range of products, most famous of which are their molded plywood designs. The Eames developed a range of chairs in this style, including the "DCW" (Dining Chair Wood) and "DCM" (Dining Chair Metal with a plywood seat) the "Eames Lounge Chair" and the "Eames Chaise", and also applied the technique to their interest in toys. The "Eames Elephant" (1945), which was designed for children to use as both a toy and a piece of furniture, is also made of plywood. Only two wooden prototypes were made, one of which was presented at the Museum of Modern Art in New York, but today it is manufactured

in plastic by the furniture house Vitra. The Eames team continued to innovate the field of design, developing new technologies for working with fiberglass, plastic resin and wire mesh. Their office maintained its success for more than 40 years, and their projects included occasional collaborations with other designers, like Charles's longtime friend Eero Saarinen.

In 1949, Charles and Ray designed and built a home for themselves in California, which became one of the most renowned post-war residences in the world. In 1979, the Royal Institute of British Architects awarded Charles and Ray Eames the Royal Gold Medal.

Charles Eames (1907–1978) und Bernice "Ray" Eames (1912–1988) waren ein amerikanisches Designer-Ehepaar, das wesentlich zur zeitgenössischen Architektur und Möbeldesign beigetragen hat.

Nach ihrer Heirat im Jahr 1941 arbeiteten sie an einer Reihe von Produkten, von denen ihre Stücke aus verformten Sperrholzplatten die berühmtesten wurden. Sie entwickelten eine Reihe von Stühlen in diesem Stil, wie z.B. den "DCW" (Esszimmerstuhl aus Holz) und den "DCM" (Esszimmerstuhl aus Metall mit einer Sperrholzsitzfläche), den "Eames Lounge Chair" (Klubsessel) und die "Eames Chaise". Sie wandten diese Methode auch auf ihre Spielzeugentwürfe an; so diente z.B. der "Eames Elefant" (1945) Kindern als Spielzeug und als Möbelstück. Es wurden von diesem "Elefant" nur zwei Prototypen hergestellt, von denen einer im Museum of Modern Art in New York ausgestellt wurde. Heutzutage wird das Modell vom Möbelhersteller Vitra aus Kunststoff angeboten. Das Ehepaar entwickelte auch moderne Methoden für die Bearbeitung von Acrylglas, Kunstharz und Drahtgeflecht.

Ihr Büro arbeitete mehr als 40 Jahre mit großem Erfolg, wobei ihre Projekte auch gelegentlich in Zusammenarbeit mit anderen Designern, wie z.B. Eero Saarinen, entstanden. 1949 entwarfen und bauten Charles und Ray ihr Eigenheim in Kalifornien, welches eines der berühmtesten Nachkriegshäuser der Welt wurde.

Im Jahr 1979 verlieh das Royal Institute of British Architects Charles und Ray Eames den Royal Gold Medal Architekturpreis.

The Molded Plywood Lounge Chair is one of the most iconic pieces of 20th century design. It has a low-slung form that relates directly to the contours of the human body.

Der Plywood Lounge Chair aus gebogenem Schichtholz ist eines der kultigsten Design-Objekte des 20. Jahrhunderts. Seine tiefliegende Form ist genau an die Anatomie des menschlichen Körpers angepasst.

The Eames Elephant was designed as a toy for children. It was originally made out of plywood, but this version never made it into mass production.

Der Eames Elefant wurde als Kinderspielzeug entworfen. Die ursprüngliche Variante aus Schichtholz wurde niemals in Serie produziert.

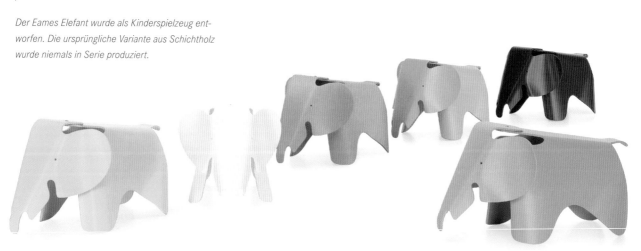

The voluptuous, organic form of La Chaise was made possible by technological advances in molding fiberglass to create free-form shells for flexible seating.

Die üppige organische Form von La Chaise entstand durch technologische Fortschritte in dem Formen von Glasfasern die es ermöglichte frei geformte Schalen für flexible Sitzmöbel zu gestalten.

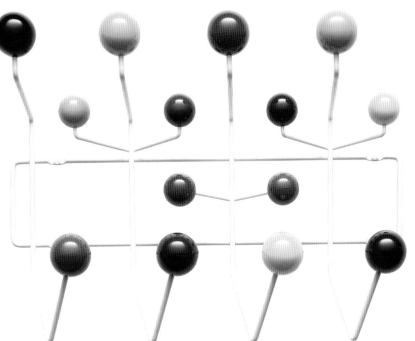

Hang-it-All brings pop colors and long-lasting function for both young and old. Great for jackets, hats, boots, backpacks, toys.

Hang-it-All bringt poppige Farben und dauerhafte Funktionalität in das Leben von Jung und Alt. Sehr gut geeignet für Jacken, Hüte, Stiefel, Rucksäcke und Spielsachen.

The Molded Plastic Side Chair with dowel-leg
base is a reproduction of the first mass-produced
molded plastic chair. Its recyclable polypropylene
seat sits on solid maple wood dowels and a steel
base.

Der Side Chair aus gegossenem Plastik mit einem
sternförmigen Holz-Untergestell ist eine Nach-
bildung des ersten in Serie produzierten Stuhls
aus gegossenem Kunststoff. Seine Polypropylen-
Sitzschale sitzt auf massiven Walnussholzstäben
mit einem Stahluntergestell.

This timeless chair is commonly referred to as the Eiffel chair; the Molded Plastic Chair was the first industrially manufactured plastic chair. It is now made out of eco-friendly polypropylene.

Dieser zeitlose Stuhl wird allgemein als Eiffel-Stuhl bezeichnet. Der Stuhl aus Plastikguss ist der erste in Serie produzierte Plastikstuhl. Heute wird er aus umweltfreundlichem Polypropylen hergestellt.

The Wire Chair with Bikini – DKR.2 is a wire shell version of the Molded Plastic chair, it has an airy silhouette with a black leather "bikini" pad and it is complemented with an "Eiffel" base.

Der Wire Chair mit Bikini – DKR.2 ist eine Drahtgestell-Version des gegossenen Plastikstuhls. Er hat eine luftige Form mit einem schwarzen Leder-„Bikini" Polsterung und einem „Eiffel" Untergestell.

The Lounge Chair and ottoman was designed as a modern answer to the Edwardian English club chair and as a gift for the Academy Award-winning director Billy Wilder, a good friend of Charles Eames.

Der Lounge Chair mit Hocker wurde als moderne Interpretation des klassischen englischen Klubsessels entworfen als Geschenk für den mit dem Academy Award ausgezeichneten Regisseur Billy Wilder, einem guten Freund von Charles Eames.

Nicknamed the "surfboard table", this elongated Elliptical Table exemplifies the delightful playfulness that enlivened and revealed the Eames' desire to create simple and beautiful furniture.

Bekannt als der „Surfbrett Tisch", verkörpert dieser gestreckte elliptische Tisch das Ziel der Eames, einfache und schöne Möbel zu entwerfen.

Also known as the Time-Life Chair, the Executive
Chair is an iconic piece originally created for
the executive floors of New York City's Time-Life
Building in 1960.

*Auch als Time-Life Chair bekannt, ist der Executive
Chair ein Kultobjekt das ursprünglich für die Chefetagen des Time-Life Building in New York 1960
entworfen wurde.*

The Walnut Stool, designed in 1960 for the lobby
of the Time Life Building in New York City, acts as
a low table or a simple seat.

*Der Walnuss Hocker, 1960 für die Lobby des Time
Life Gebäude in New York City entworfen, kann
als niedriger Tisch oder einfacher Sitz verwendet
werden.*

The Aluminum Chairs, designed in 1958, might well be the Eames' most famous creations, and they are certainly among the most important designs of the 20th century.

Die Aluminium Chairs, entworfen 1958, sind wahrscheinlich die berühmteste Arbeit der Eames und sind sicherlich einige der bedeutendsten Designs des 20. Jahrhunderts.

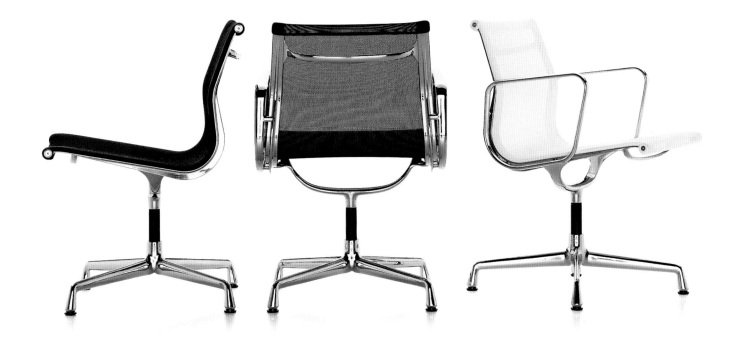

The simple design leaves the structure visible and easy to understand, and much of the chairs' acclaim is due to the clever use of materials. Aluminum keeps the chair lightweight and comfortable.

Durch das klare Design bleibt die Struktur sichtbar und leicht verständlich. Die intelligente Verwendung des Materials trug maßgeblich zu der Bekanntheit des Stuhles bei. Durch die Verwendung von Aluminium ist der Stuhl leicht und bequem.

The Tulip Chair rests gracefully on a pedestal, thus ending the problem of crowded chair legs under a table. The curved shell cradles the sitter's body and includes armrests.

Der Tulip Chair sitzt graziös auf einem Sockel, womit das Problem von Stuhlbein-Chaos unter dem Tisch gelöst ist. Die gebogene Schale umschmeichelt den Körper und bildet gleichzeitig Armlehnen.

Eero Saarinen

Eero Saarinen (August 20, 1910 – September 1, 1961) was a Finnish-American architect and industrial designer whose ability to switch between different styles depending on the demands of each project made him one of the most versatile designers of the 20th century.

The son of the architect Eliel Saarinen, Eero took courses in sculpture and furniture design at the Cranbrook Academy of Art, where his father taught, and where he developed a close friendship with fellow students Charles and Ray Eames. In 1929, he went on to study sculpture in Paris and then attended the Yale School of Architecture. From 1940 to 1944, Saarinen was recruited by the military to draw illustrations for bomb disassembly manuals and to provide designs for the White House Situation Room.

Saarinen began an extended and very successful association with the Knoll furniture company in the 1940s, which resulted in some of his most famous furniture pieces, including the "Womb" series and the world-famous "Tulip Chair", which was featured on the original Star Trek television series. Saarinen also received enormous recognition as an architect after designing the Gateway Arch in St. Louis, Missouri and the main terminal of the Dulles International Airport near Washington D.C.

Eero Saarinen (20.8.1910–1.9.1961) war ein finnisch-amerikanischer Architekt und Industriedesigner, dessen Fähigkeit, zwischen verschiedenen Stilrichtungen je nach den Erfordernissen des Projektes zu wechseln, ihn zu einem der vielseitigsten Designer des 20. Jahrhunderts machte.

Eero war der Sohn des Architekten Eliel Saarinen. Er studierte Bildhauerei und Möbeldesign an der Cranbrook Academy of Art, wo sein Vater unterrichtete; dort schloss er eine enge Freundschaft mit seinen Kommilitonen Charles und Ray Eames. 1929 ging er nach Paris, um dort weiterhin Bildhauerei zu studieren, und besuchte dann die Yale School of Architecture. Von 1940 bis 1944 wurde Saarinen vom amerikanischen Militär beauftragt, Illustrationen für Bombenentschärfungsanleitungen zu zeichnen sowie Entwürfe für den „Situations Room" (Kontrollraum) im Weißen Haus zu liefern.

In den 1940ern begann Saarinen eine langfristige und sehr produktive Zusammenarbeit mit der Möbelfirma Knoll, der einige seiner berühmtesten Möbelstücke entsprangen, wie z. B. die „Womb" (Gebärmutter)-Serie und der weltberühmte „Tulpenstuhl", der in der Fernsehserie „Raumschiff Enterprise" zu sehen war. Saarinen wurde außerdem als Architekt sehr berühmt durch seinen Entwurf des Gateway Arch, dem Wahrzeichen von St. Louis in Missouri, sowie dem Hauptterminal des Dulles International Airport in der Nähe von Washington D.C.

The Conference Chair benefits from Saarinen's revolutionary use of molded fiberglass, creating a more flexible shell that responds to the weight of the occupant.

Der Konferenzstuhl profitiert von Saarinens revolutionärer Handhabung von geformten Glasfasern, wodurch eine flexiblere Schale entsteht die sich dem Gewicht des Nutzers anpasst.

For the Womb Chair, thick foam padding is added on top of the fiberglass chair, providing unparalleled comfort. Two extra cushions and a matching ottoman completes the sculptural creation.

Für den Womb Chair wurde eine dicke Schaumpolsterung auf den Glasfaserstuhl aufgelegt womit der Sessel beispiellos gemütlich wurde. Zwei zusätzliche Kissen sowie ein passender Hocker vervollständigen die skulpturale Kreation.

THE MUSEUM OF CONTEMPORARY ART LOS ANGELES

The CH28 armchair was originally made in oak and teak, although the latter has now been replaced by walnut. The rounded armrests and back provide comfort as well as an elegant, organic look.

Ursprünglich wurde der Sessel CH28 aus Eiche und Teakholz hergestellt, letzeres wurde durch Walnuss ersetzt. Die gerundeten Armlehnen und Rücken bieten Komfort mit einer eleganten, natürlichen Optik.

Hans J. Wegner

Hans Wegner (April 2, 1914 – January 26, 2007) was a Danish furniture designer of the Modernist school, whose functional chairs contributed to the popularity of Danish design in the mid 20th century.

After an apprenticeship with a cabinet-maker in his hometown, Wegner studied at the Danish School of Arts and Crafts and the Architectural Academy in Copenhagen. In 1938, he presented a dining table, chairs and armchairs at the Snedkerlaugets exhibition in Copenhagen, already displaying the stripped-down aesthetic that would characterize much of his career. In 1940, Wegner started working for Arne Jacobsen's architecture studio, where he was in charge of designing the furniture for the Århus Municipal Hall. He then started his own company, and began a very successful independent career, creating over 500 different chair designs for furniture companies like Carl Hansen & Son, Fritz Hansen, Getama, and Møbler.

His timeless designs are marked by a deep understanding and appreciation for wood as a material, and his eye for detail in terms of construction clearly stems from his carpentry training. The curved wood of the "Shell" chair and the ingenious storage space and coat hanger included in the "Valet" chair bear witness to his technical skill as well as his creativity. Over the course of his career, Wegner received a number of prizes and awards, including the Grand Prix of the Milan Triennale in 1951 and the Danish Eckersberg Medal.

Hans Wegner (2.4.1914–26.1.2007) war ein dänischer Möbeldesigner der Moderne, dessen funktionelle Stühle zur Beliebtheit von dänischem Design Mitte des 20. Jahrhunderts beigetragen haben.

Nach einer Tischlerlehre in seinem Heimatort studierte Wegner an der Kunsthandwerkerschule in Kopenhagen. 1938 präsentierte er in der Snedkerlaugets Ausstellung in Kopenhagen einen Esstisch, Stühle und Sessel, die schon die schlichte Ästhetik vorwiesen, die den größten Teil seiner Arbeiten charakterisiert. 1940 begann Wegner für das Architekturstudio von Arne Jacobsen zu arbeiten, wo er für den Entwurf der Möbel für das Rathaus von Aarhus zuständig war. Er gründete daraufhin seine eigene Firma und begann eine sehr erfolgreiche Karriere, während der er für Möbelhersteller wie Carl Hansen & Son, Fritz Hansen, Getama, und Møbler über 500 verschiedene Stühle entwarf.

Seine zeitlosen Designs sind geprägt von einem tiefen Verständnis und der Würdigung des Materials Holz sowie seinem Blick für bauliche Details, die von seinem Können als Tischler herrühren. Das gebogene Holz des Stuhls „Shell" sowie die geniale Staufläche und Kleiderbügel des Stuhls „Valet" bezeugen sein technisches Können und seine Kreativität.

Im Laufe seiner Karriere erhielt Wegner viele Auszeichnungen und Preise, wie z.B. den Grand Prix der Triennale di Milano in 1951 und die dänische Eckersberg Medaille.

The AT 319 dinner table is one of the results of
Wegner's experiments with wood and steel. The
tabletop, originally made of solid ash wood, rests
on four slender steel legs.

*Der Esstisch AT 319 ist ein Resultat von Wegner's
Experimenten mit Holz und Stahl. Die Tischplatte,
ursprünglich aus massiver Esche, ruht auf vier
schlanken Beinen.*

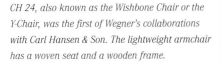

CH 24, also known as the Wishbone Chair or the Y-Chair, was the first of Wegner's collaborations with Carl Hansen & Son. The lightweight armchair has a woven seat and a wooden frame.

CH 24, auch bekannt unter den Namen Wishbone Chair oder Y-Chair, war eine der ersten gemeinsamen Arbeiten von Wegner mit Carl Hansen & Son. Der leichte Sessel hat einen gewebten Sitz und eine Holzrahmen.

The three-legged CH 07 lounge chair is a true feat of design and carpentry. The front two legs are one continuous piece of laminated construction, and the seat and backrest are pressed plywood shells.

Der dreibeinige Klubsessel CH 07 ist ein echtes Design und Tischlerei Meisterstück. Die beiden vorderen Beine bestehen aus einem durchgängigen Stück laminiertem Holz, während der Sitz und Rückenlehne aus gepressten Schichtholzschalen bestehen.

The China Chair got its name from the 17th and 18th century Chinese chairs that inspired its design. The detailed carving and harmonious lines of this chair exemplify Wegner's talent as a carpenter.

Der China Chair erhielt seinen Namen von den chinesischen Stühlen des 17. und 18. Jahrhunderts, die als Inspiration dienten. Die detaillierten Schnitzereien und harmonischen Linien dieses Stuhls beweisen Wegners Tischlertalent.

PP 501, which Wegner referred to as, "The round one," is arguably his ~~most~~ famous creation. PP 503 differs only in that it is upholstered. The simple designed has earned his chair lasting popularity.

PP 501, den Wegner „The round one" nannte, ist wohl sein berühmtestes Werk. PP 503 unterscheidet sich nur durch seine Polsterung. Das schlichte Design machte den Stuhl durchgehend beliebt.

The minimalist PP 586 tray is produced in either ash or mahogany, and marks a rare departure from Wegner's usual work in more substantial furniture.

Die minimalistische Servier- oder Obstschale PP 586 wird aus Esche oder Mahagoni hergestellt und ist eine seltene Ausnahme von Wegners meist voluminöseren Möbeldesigns.

PP 550, better known as the Peacock Chair, is both aesthetically and practically designed. The flat pieces of the wooden rods that form the back-rest are placed at shoulder level, for maximum comfort.

PP 550, besser bekannt als der Peacock Chair hat ein gleichzeitig praktisches und ästhetisches Design. Die flachen Teile der Holzstäbe die den Rücken bilden sind auf Schulterhöhe platziert für optimalen Komfort.

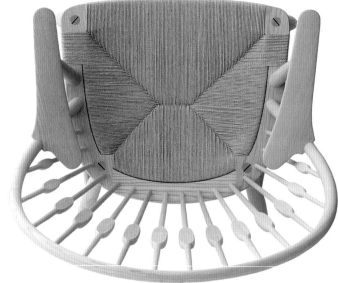

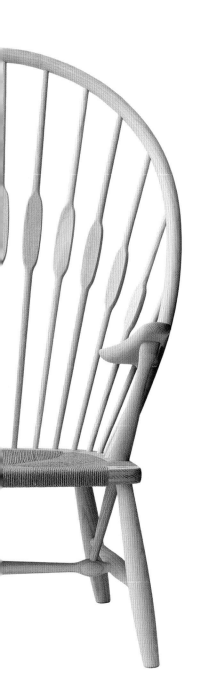

CH 29 is one of Wegner's more innovative designs. The legs extend up to form the frame, allowing the use of fewer parts, and the wide seat and curved backrest make it especially comfortable.

CH 29 ist eines von Wegners innovativeren Designs. Die Beine reichen empor um den Rahmen zu bilden, womit Teile eingespart werden, während der breite Sitz und ein gebogenes Rückenteil ihn besonders bequem machen.

The Bull Chair's top rail is more heavily emphasized than usual, giving it the playful appearance of a bull's horns. The wooden chair features a woven seat and a carved detail in the backrest.

Die obere Lehne des Bull Chair ist stärker als üblich hervorgehoben, was ihr den spielerischen Anschein von Stierhörnern gibt. Der hölzerne Stuhl hat einen gewebten Sitz und eine Schnitzerei im Rücken.

Bertoia's Side Chair is made of welded steel, but maintains a lightweight feel and an almost delicate aesthetic.

Bertoias Side Chair besteht aus geschweißtem Stahl, weckt aber ein Gefühl von Leichtigkeit mit einer fast zerbrechlich anmutenden Ästhetik.

Harry
Bertoia

Harry Bertoia (March 10, 1915 – November 6, 1978) was an Italian-born sculptor, and furniture designer. He studied design and handmade jewelry making at the Cass Technical High School in Detroit, then received a scholarship to study at the Cranbrook Academy of Art. Eero Saarinen, another Cranbrook alumni, later commissioned him to design a metal screen for the General Motors Technical Center in Detroit.

After working for a number of years in jewelry making, Bertoia started applying his knowledge of metal work and sculpture to furniture design. Working with Knoll, he created five wire pieces now known as the "Bertoia Collection", effectively transforming industrial wire rods into an iconic design element. The collection showcased his skilled use of metal latticework, as well as his unique sculptural sensibility. Following the success of this collection, Bertoia was able to devote himself entirely to sculpture. In particular, Bertoia became interested in "Sound Sculpture", in which he manipulated metal to produce sound, so that it would respond in different tones to wind, vibrations, or touch.

Harry Bertoia (10.3.1915–6.11.1978) war ein aus Italien stammender Bildhauer und Möbel-Designer. Er studierte Design und Schmuckherstellung an der Cass Technical High School in Detroit und erhielt dann ein Stipendium für die Cranbrook Academy of Art. Eero Saarinen, ein weiterer Cranbrook-Absolvent, beauftragte ihn später mit dem Entwurf für eine Metallabschirmung für das General Motors Technikzentrum in Detroit.

Nachdem er längere Zeit in der Schmuckherstellung tätig war, wendete Bertoia seine Erfahrungen in der Arbeit mit Metall und in der Bildhauerei für den Entwurf von Möbeln an. In Zusammenarbeit mit Knoll erschuf er fünf Stücke aus Draht, die als die „Bertoia-Sammlung" bekannt wurden. Er nutzte hierbei industriellen Walzdraht als ein einzigartiges Designelement. Die Sammlung zeigt seine große Kunstfertigkeit in der Bearbeitung von Metallgitterwerk sowie seine einzigartige bildhauerische Sensibilität. Durch den großen Erfolg dieser Sammlung konnte Bertoia sich ganz auf die Bildhauerei konzentrieren. Er interessierte sich besonders für den Bereich „Tonskulptur", wobei er Metall so bearbeitete, dass es Töne erzeugte und in verschieden Tonlagen auf Wind, Vibrationen oder Berührungen reagierte.

Bertoia's striking metal chair series includes the
diamond chair, the bird chair and ottoman, and
the side chair and bar stool. All of the chairs can
be upholstered.

*Zu Bertoias beeindruckender Metallstuhl-
Kollektion gehören der Stuhl Diamond, der Stuhl
und die Ottomane Bird sowie der Side Stuhl und
Barhocker.*

The Diamond chairs' metal rods are so thin that,
in Bertoia's own words, "they are mainly made
out of air. like sculpture. Space passes right
through them."

*Die Metallstäbe des Stuhls Diamond sind so dünn,
dass sie nach Bertoias eigenen Worten „hauptsächlich aus Luft bestehen, wie eine Skulptur. Der
Raum geht glatt durch sie hindurch."*

Meaning "sharecropper" in Italian, Mezzadro is
made of a chromium-plated steel stem, steam-
treated beech footrest in a natural finish, and
aluminum seat lacquered in six vibrant colors.

Der Name Mezzadro kommt aus dem Italienischen
und bedeutet „Farmpächter". Der Stuhl besteht
aus einem verchromten Stahlfuß, einer Fußstütze
aus Buche sowie einer Aluminiumsitzfläche, die an
einen Traktorsitz erinnert und in sechs leuchtenden Farben lackiert ist.

Achille
Castiglioni

Achille Castiglioni (February 16, 1918 – December 6, 2002) was an influential Italian designer of the 20th century. In 1944, after graduating from the Polytechnic Institute of Milan with a degree in architecture, he opened a design office with his two brothers. Together, the brothers experimented with new production techniques and materials, and developed the process of "Integral Design" which Achille summed up with the famous quote, "Start from scratch. Stick to common sense. Know your goals and means." In his view, good design leads to innovation in the production process as well as in the final product itself. Much of Castiglioni's work also focused on the re-purposing objects, which can best be seen in the "Sella" and "Mezzadro" chairs. "Sella" uses a bicycle saddle, and Mezzadro is made using a tractor seat.

His works were exhibited at every Milan Triennial since 1947, and he won seven Compasso d'Oro awards during the course of his career, for products as diverse as cutlery, espresso machines, earphones, and lamps. Some of his designs are included in the permanent collection of the Museum of Modern Art in New York. In addition to producing his own projects, Castiglioni also made a career of teaching, leading classes at the Polytechnic University of Turin and then Milan.

Achille Castiglioni (16.2.1918–6.12.2002) war ein einflussreicher italienischer Designer des 20. Jahrhunderts.

Nach Abschluss seines Architekturstudiums an der Polytechnischen Universität von Mailand eröffnete er zusammen mit seinen zwei Brüdern ein Designbüro. Außerdem arbeitete Castiglioni auch als Dozent an der Polytechnischen Universität von Turin und später der von Mailand. Gemeinsam mit seinen Brüdern experimentierte er mit neuen Produktionsmethoden und -materialien; sie entwickelten die „Integral Design"-Methode, welche Achille in dem berühmten Zitat zusammenfasste: „Fange bei Null an. Halte dich an den gesunden Menschenverstand. Kenne deine Ziele und Möglichkeiten." Seiner Ansicht nach führt gutes Design zu innovativen Produktionsabläufen und innovativen Endprodukten. Ein großer Teil von Castiglionis Arbeit beinhaltete auch die Umnutzung von Dingen, wovon die besten Beispiele die Stühle „Sella" und „Mezzadro" sind: Für „Sella" wurde ein Fahrradsattel verwendet, während „Mezzadro" aus einem Traktorsitz hergestellt wurde.

Seine Arbeiten wurden auf jeder Triennalo di Milano-Ausstellung seit 1947 gezeigt. Er gewann im Lauf seiner Karriere sieben Mal den Compasso d'Oro für so unterschiedliche Produkte wie Besteck, Espresso-Maschinen, Kopfhörer und Leuchten. Einige seiner Designs sind Teil der ständigen Sammlung des Museum of Modern Art in New York.

Sella's seat is a black racing bicycle saddle with
pink lacquered steel column and cast iron base.

Sella besteht aus einem schwarzen Rennradsattel
als Sitz mit einer rosa lackierten Stahlstange und
gusseisernem Sockel.

The 360 Servomuto has a polypropylene base and a steel rod. Its top comes in black or white layered, plastic laminate.

Der 360 Servomuto besteht aus einem Polypropylen-Sockel und einem Stahlstab. Seine Platte ist beschichtet mit schwarzem oder weißem, mehrlagigem HPL.

Designed without traditional padding in order to lay bare the essential curves that are "strictly necessary" to ensure optimal support, Sanluca is an extraordinary example of an ergonomic armchair.

Durch den Verzicht auf konventionelle Polsterung ist Sanluca ein außergewöhnliches Beispiel eines ergonomischen Sessels; damit sollen die wesentlichen Kurven gezeigt werden, die "grundsätzlich nötig" sind, um optimalen Halt zu geben.

Leonardo is a working table with adjustable height. It has a natural varnished steam-treated beech trestle and the top is coated with either white plastic laminate or tempered plate glass.

Leonardo ist ein Arbeitstisch mit verstellbarer Höhe. Sein Gestell besteht aus lackierter, dampfbehandelter Buche, während die Arbeitsplatte entweder mit weißem HPL oder mit Hartglas bedeckt ist.

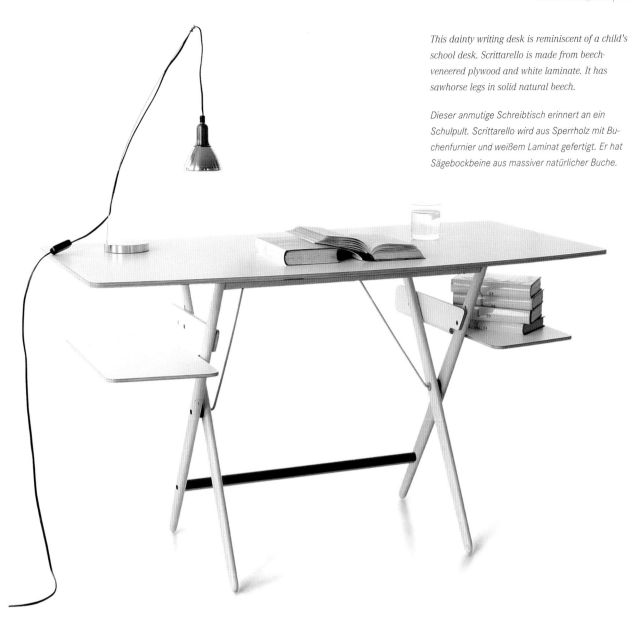

This dainty writing desk is reminiscent of a child's school desk. Scrittarello is made from beech-veneered plywood and white laminate. It has sawhorse legs in solid natural beech.

Dieser anmutige Schreibtisch erinnert an ein Schulpult. Scrittarello wird aus Sperrholz mit Buchenfurnier und weißem Laminat gefertigt. Er hat Sägebockbeine aus massiver natürlicher Buche.

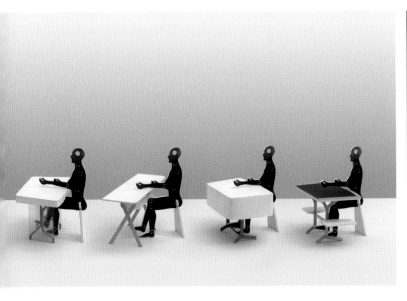

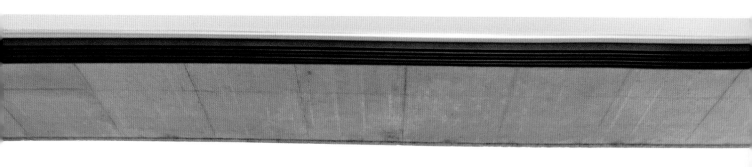

The USM Modular Furniture System Haller is a system of shelves, drawers, and tables whose design was inspired by modular architectural constructions.

Das USM Möbelbausystem Haller besteht aus Regalen, Schubladen und Tischen, deren Design von modularen architektonischen Entwürfen geprägt wurde.

Fritz Paul
Haller Schärer

Fritz Haller (born October 23, 1924 in So-lothurn) is a Swiss architect and designer. After an apprenticeship as a carpenter, he worked in several architecture offices in Switzerland and then in the Netherlands, before establishing himself as an architect in his own right. In 1963, Haller collabo-rated with the engineer Paul Schärer (born in 1933 in Bern) and Schärer's family busi-ness, USM, to develop the USM Modular Furniture System Haller. This collection of modular furniture, which was initially just meant for the USM offices, was first mass-produced in 1969, and was an instant worldwide hit. The furniture system was inspired by modular architecture, with the creed "Form follows Function" guiding the skeletal design. The initial system of storage units, with a structure of chromed steel tub-ing connected to brass ball joints, featured a set of standard components that could be set up according to the needs of each individual user. A set of multi-functional tables was designed next, which perfectly complemented the storage system. Today, the USM Haller range is considered a 20th century design classic, and is featured in the permanent collection of the Museum of Modern Art in New York.

Fritz Haller (geb. 23.10.1924 in Solothurn) ist ein Schweizer Architekt und Designer. Nach einer Berufslehre als Zimmermann ar-beitete er für verschiedene Architekturbüros in der Schweiz und Holland, bevor er sich als Architekt selbstständig machte.

1963 entwickelte Haller zusammen mit dem Ingenieur Paul Schärer (geb. 1933 in Bern) und Schärers Familienunternehmen USM das USM Möbelbausystem Haller. Diese Reihe von modularen Möbelelemen-ten, die zunächst nur für die USM Büros bestimmt war, wurde 1969 zum ersten Mal serienmäßig produziert und war sofort inter-national sehr gefragt. Das Möbelbausystem wurde vom architektonischen Baukasten-prinzip inspiriert, dessen Design auf dem Leitsatz „Form folgt Funktion" basiert. Aus dem Basissystem von Regal- und Schrank-elementen aus zusammenschraubbaren, verchromten Stahlrohren mit Messingku-gelgelenken lassen sich individuelle Objekte und Kombinationen bauen. Eine Reihe von Multifunktionstischen, die das System per-fekt ergänzen, kam als nächstes dazu.

Heute ist das USM Möbelbausystem Haller ein Design-Klassiker des 20. Jahrhun-derts und wurde in die permanente Samm-lung des Museum of Modern Art in New York aufgenommen.

The modular elements of the system are stackable
and combinable, allowing endless customization
and expansion.

Die baukastenähnlichen Elemente des Systems
sind stapel- und kombinierbar, was unendliche An-
passungs- und Erweiterungsmöglichkeiten bietet.

The Modular Furniture System was initially
conceived for offices, but it was launched on the
market in 1965. It has since found a place in
homes, libraries, and more.

Das Möbelbausystem wurde ursprünglich für Büros
entworfen und 1965 auf dem Markt eingeführt.
Seit dieser Zeit hat es auch einen festen Platz
in Privatwohnungen, Bibliotheken und
anderen Orten gefunden.

The revolutionary Panton Chair was the first
single-injection molded-plastic chair. It went into
mass production in 1967, and instantly became
an icon of 20th century furniture design.

Der revolutionäre Panton Stuhl war der erste aus
einem einzigen Stück Polypropylen gezogene
Kunststoffstuhl. 1967 wurde er das erste mal in
Serie produziert und zählt seitdem als Kultobjekt
des 20. Jahrhunderts.

Verner Panton

Verner Panton (February 13, 1926 – September 5, 1998) was one of the most influential Danish designers of the 20th century, whose wide range of imaginative and futuristic designs earned him both acclaim and controversy throughout his career. After studying as an architectural engineer at a technical college in Odense and then at the Royal Danish Academy of Fine Arts in Copenhagen, he worked in Arne Jacobsen's architectural office from 1950–1952, and started his own office in 1955. His first architectural projects were quite controversial, and included a collapsible house, a cardboard house, and a house made out of plastic. He extended this boundless creativity to his furniture design, creating pieces with unconventional shapes, or which seemed to be missing traditional elements.

The "Cone chair", for example, has no discernible legs or backrest, and seems almost to float, unsupported, in space. In 1960, he became the first designer to create the single-injection molded plastic chair. Rejecting traditional functionalism, Panton saw a set of furniture as a landscape, which should be able to exist for its own sake and "interact with itself." In the 1960s and 1970s, he went on to design entire environments, furnished completely with his own curved furniture and decorated with psychedelic circular patterns. His bold designs, with their fantastical forms and beautiful colors, remain very popular today.

Verner Panton (13.2.1926–5.9.1998) war einer der einflussreichsten dänischen Designer des 20. Jahrhunderts. Seine große Vielfalt an phantasievollen und futuristischen Entwürfen war manchmal kontrovers, aber immer hoch gelobt. Nach einem Ingenieurstudium an der Technischen Hochschule in Odense und der Königlich Dänischen Kunstakademie in Kopenhagen arbeitete er im Architekturbüro von Arne Jacobsen und gründete 1955 sein eigenes Büro.

Seine ersten architektonischen Projekte, unter anderem ein zusammenlegbares Haus, ein Kartonhaus und ein Haus aus Plastik, waren recht kontrovers. Er übertrug seine grenzenlose Kreativität dann auf Möbelentwürfe und erschuf Objekte mit ungewöhnlichen Formen oder mit scheinbar fehlenden traditionellen Elementen. Der Tütenstuhl „Cone chair" z. B. hat keine erkennbaren Beine oder Rückenlehne und scheint fast eigenständig in der Luft zu schweben. 1960 war Panton der erste Designer, der einen Kunststoffstuhl aus einem Guss erschuf. Panton lehnte traditionellen Funktionalismus ab und betrachtete eine Möbelgruppe als eine Landschaft, die autark existieren konnte und sich „mit sich selbst auseinandersetzte". In den 1960er und 70er Jahren begann er ganze Landschaften zu konzipieren, die komplett mit seinen eigenen kurvenförmigen Möbeln ausgestattet und mit psychedelischen, runden Mustern geschmückt waren. Seine kühnen Designs mit ihren phantastischen Formen und wunderschönen Farben sind heute noch sehr beliebt.

The gravity-defying Cone Chair caused a sensation when it was first displayed in a New York City shop window – police had to disperse the crowd of shocked onlookers. The Heart Cone Chair soon followed.

Der ungewöhnlich geformte Tütenstuhl Cone Chair war eine Sensation als er das erste Mal in einem New Yorker Schaufenster ausgestellt wurde – die Polizei musste den Trauben von geschockten Zuschauern auflösen. Der Heart Cone Chair wurde bald darauf entwickelt

The Living Tower was one of Panton's "Living Landscapes." Several meters high, it allows a number of different seating or reclining possibilities. The idea was that this furniture could be lived in.

Der Living Tower war eine von Pantons „Wohnland-schaften". Er ermöglicht eine Reihe von Sitz- oder Liegemöglichkeiten mit der Idee, dass man in diesem Möbelstück leben kann.

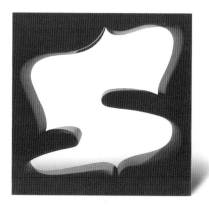

The Relaxer Chair is a rocking chair that is
formed from one fluid, sweeping curve of wood.
The chair sits low to the ground, and the curve fits
virtually any body and posture.

Der Schaukelstuhl Relaxer ist aus einem einzigen
gewölbten Stück Holz geformt. Der Stuhl ist niedrig
konzipiert und seine Wölbung passt zu praktisch
jeder Anatomie und Körperhaltung.

The contours of the Orange Slice Chair curl up invitingly, and the shape seems different from every angle. Paulin's signature foam and fabric shell rests on a slender, tubular steel frame.

Die Konturen des Sessels Orange Slice sind einladend nach oben gebogen und seine Form erscheint von jedem Blickwinkel anders. Zwei identisch geformte Schalen ruhen auf einem schlanken Stahlrohrrahmen.

Pierre
Paulin

Pierre Paulin (July 9, 1927 – June 13, 2009) was a French designer, most renowned for his series of foam chairs, whose Pop aesthetic made them instant icons of 1960s design. Paulin had initially intended to become a sculptor, attending an art school in Paris, but soon turned to furniture design instead. He exhibited his first creations, a series of discreet, wooden pieces that were designed to fit multi-functional environments, at a design fair in Paris in 1953, and in 1956, he joined the furniture design company Artifort. By the 1960s, he was pioneering new technologies and materials, creating expansive, multi-layered chairs with no discernible frame, upholstered in bright colors and soft material. The foam structures were as supportive as traditional materials, but much more animated, as the material could easily take on increasingly abstract shapes. As the shapes became more and more fantastical, Paulin collaborated with textile designers to create new textile concepts that could stretch over the irregular structures, eventually settling on brightly colored and patterned jersey material, also an innovation at the time. This departure from traditional rigidity in form and design was a perfect fit for the 1960s, and brought him great commercial success.

Pierre Paulin (9.7.1927–13.6.2009) war ein französischer Designer, der vor allem für seine Schaumstoffsessel bekannt war, deren Pop-Ästhetik sie sofort zu Kultobjekten der Design-Szene der 1960er Jahre machte. Paulin wollte ursprünglich Bildhauer werden und besuchte eine Kunstakademie in Paris, wandte sich aber bald dem Möbeldesign zu.

Er stellte 1953 seine ersten Arbeiten, diskrete Holzmöbel, die multifunktionalen Ansprüchen gerecht wurden, auf einer Designermesse in Paris aus. 1956 begann er für die Möbeldesignfirma Artifort zu arbeiten. In den sechziger Jahren war er ein Wegbereiter für die Arbeit mit neuen Methoden und Materialien, mit deren Hilfe er großformatige mehrlagige Sessel ohne erkennbaren Rahmen in kräftigen Farben, gepolstert mit weichem Stoff, schuf. Die Schaumstoffstrukturen boten den gleichen Halt wie traditionelle Materialien, waren aber viel kreativer, da sie zunehmend abstraktere Formen annehmen konnten. Als die Formen immer phantastischer wurden, arbeitete Paulin mit Stoffdesignern zusammen, um neue Stoffkonzepte zu entwickeln, die über die ungleichförmigen Strukturen gezogen werden konnten. Letztendlich entschied er sich für farbenkräftige, bunt gemusterte Stretchstoffe, was ebenfalls eine absolute Innovation zu dieser Zeit war.

Diese Abkehr von traditionell vorgegebenen Formen und Designs passte perfekt zu den 1960ern und brachte ihm großen kommerziellen Erfolg ein.

*At first glance, the Oyster Chair seems more geo-
metric than Paulin's other designs, but the lines
are softened and slightly curved, maintaining his
warm aesthetic.*

*Auf den ersten Blick erscheint der Sessel Oyster
geradliniger als Paulins andere Entwürfe, er sorgt
aber durch weiche Linien und eine leichte Wölbung
für eine warme Ästhctik.*

The Butterfly Chair rests on an origami-like, tubular steel frame, and is made either of leather or cowhide instead of the usual foam.

Der Butterfly Chair ruht auf einem Stahlrohrrahmen der an Origami erinnert und ist aus Leder oder Rindsleder anstatt dem üblichen Schaum.

The Mushroom Chair's single, sculptural form rises up from the ground like its namesake. The open, rounded seat allows great freedom of movement as well as comfort.

Die skulpturale Form des Mushroom Sessels wächst aus dem Boden wie sein Namensvetter. Der offene abgerundete Sitz bietet große Bewegungsfreiheit und Komfort.

The Tongue Chair is surely Paulin's boldest and most playful design. The sitter lounge back on a curved, lolling tongue, and the flowing shape has made the chair an icon of 1960s design.

Der Tongue Chair ist sicherlich Paulins gewagtestes und verspieltestes Design. Der Benutzer lehnt sich zurück auf einer gebogenen, herausgestreckten Zunge. Seine fließende Form machte den Stuhl in den 1960er Jahren legendär.

The Ribbon Chair rolls back under itself, so that the backrest, the seat, and the legs are all part of one continuous form, for a design that is both bold and graceful.

Der Ribbon Chair ist unter sich eingerollt, wodurch die Rückenlehne, der Sitz und die Beine alles Komponenten einer einzigen durchgängigen Form sind, als Teil eines gewagten und anmutigen Designs.

The Little Tulip Chair is a fun take on the traditional office chair. The low back and petal-like armrests are just as functional as they are whimsical.

Der Little Tulip Chair ist eine verspielte Variante des traditionellen Bürostuhls. Der niedrige Rücken und Blütenblätter-ähnliche Armlehnen sind ebenso praktisch wie skurril.

Before he became so devoted to the Pop aesthetic of his later designs, Paulin created Tanis, whose minimalist steel and wood forms seem to channel the Bauhaus movement.

Bevor er sich der Pop-Ästhetik seiner späteren Arbeiten widmete, erschuf Paulin Tanis, dessen minimalistische Stahl- und Holzformen die Bauhaus-Bewegung zu verkörpern scheinen.

The shape of the PK22 lounge chair's steel frame
was actually a continuation of Kjærholm's gradu-
ation project for the School of Applied Arts in
Copenhagen.

*Die Form des Stahlrahmens des Klubsessels PK22
war eigentlich eine Fortsetzung von Kjærholms
Abschlussprojekt an der Kunstgewerbeschule in
Kopenhagen.*

Poul
Kjærholm

Poul Kjærholm (January 8, 1929 – April 18, 1980) was one of the leading forces of 20th century Danish design. After training as a carpenter, he went on to study furniture design at the Danish School of Arts and Crafts in Copenhagen, graduating in 1952. Despite his background in woodwork, Kjærholm had a keen interest in many different materials, including steel. The "PK 25" chair, which he designed in 1951 as his graduation project, displays both his skilled craftsmanship and his interest in more industrial techniques. The frame is made of chromium-plated steel that is simply bent into the final shape, with no joints needed, and the seat itself is made of cable that is wrapped around the frame. Kjærholm favored functionalism's clean lines and understated forms, which made his daring use of industrial materials and technology stand out even more. In 1973, he was made the head of the Danish Institute for Design, and in 1976 he became a professor. Kjærholm enjoyed great success throughout his career. He won the Grand Prize at the Milan Triennial in 1957 and 1960, and many of his designs were included in museum exhibits around the world, like the V&A Museum in London and the Museum of Modern Art in New York.

Poul Kjærholm (8.1.1929–18.4.1980) war einer der wichtigsten Vertreter dänischen Designs im 20. Jahrhundert. Nach einer Tischlerlehre studierte er bis 1952 Möbeldesign an der Kunstgewerbeschule in Kopenhagen.

Trotz seiner Erfahrung in der Arbeit mit Holz hatte Kjærholm großes Interesse an vielen verschiedenen Materialien, unter anderem an Stahl. Der Stuhl „PK 25", den er 1951 als seine Diplomarbeit entwarf, war ein Beispiel für seine handwerkliche Kunst, gepaart mit seinem Interesse an industriellen Techniken. Der Rahmen besteht aus verchromtem Flachstahl, der einfach fugenlos in seine endgültige Form gebogen wurde, während die Sitzfläche aus einer um den Rahmen gewickelten und gespannten Fahnenschnur besteht. Kjærholm bevorzugte die klaren Linien und unaufdringlichen Formen des Funktionalismus, was seine kühne Handhabung industrieller Materialien und Technologien noch mehr unterstrich.

1973 wurde er zum Leiter des Danish Institute for Design ernannt und 1976 wurde er Professor. Kjærholm hatte eine sehr erfolgreiche Karriere. Er gewann den Grand Prize der Triennale di Milano 1957 und 1960; viele seiner Arbeiten wurden in Museen weltweit ausgestellt, unter anderen im V&A Museum in London und im Museum of Modern Art in New York.

PK24 was inspired by French Rococo-style lounge chairs, but here the long curve of the leather seat rests on a boxy metal frame.

PK24 wurde von französischen Sesseln des Rokokostils inspiriert; hier aber ruht die lange Wölbung des Ledersitzes auf einem würfelartigen Metallrahmen.

The PK91 folding stool's X-shaped base folds neatly up, folding the leather or canvas seat neatly in two.

Das X-förmige Untergestell des Klapphockers PK91 klappt präzise nach oben, um die Leder- oder Stoffsitzfläche in zwei genaue Hälften zu teilen.

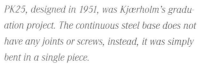

PK25, designed in 1951, was Kjærholm's gradu-ation project. The continuous steel base does not have any joints or screws, instead, it was simply bent in a single piece.

PK25, 1951 entworfen, war Kjærholms Abschluss-projekt. Das durchgängige Stahluntergestell hat keine Anschlüsse oder Schrauben, sondern wurde einfach aus einem einzelnen Stück gebogen.

Pk31 comes as an easy chair and as a sofa. The highly geometric chair sits tilted back on a steel frame.

Pk31 gibt es als Polstersessel oder Sofa. Die stark geometrische Form sitzt angewinkelt auf einem Stahlrahmen.

The PK54 dining table plays with materials as
well as forms. A circular table top is placed on
a square frame, and the heavy marble contrasts
with the metal below.

Der Esstisch PK54 spielt mit Materialien und
Formen. Eine runde Tischplatte sitzt auf einem
quadratischen Rahmen, während der schwere
Marmor mit dem Metall darunter kontrastiert.

The PK80 daybed's simple, bent steel frame is clearly inspired by the clean functionalism of the Bauhaus movement. The low daybed is upholstered in leather.

Die schlichte, gewinkelte Stahlform des Daybed PK80 ist eindeutig von dem klaren Funktionalismus der Bauhaus-Bewegung inspiriert. Die niedrige Bettcouch ist mit Leder bezogen.

The PK20 was originally conceived using leather strips left over from other designs, as a means of optimizing production. Eventually, the decision was made to only use high-quality leather or wicker.

Der PK20 wurde ursprünglich aus Lederresten von anderen Designs geschaffen, um die Produktion zu optimieren. Später wurde entschieden, nur hochwertiges Leder oder Korbmaterial für ihn zu verwenden.

Lounge Chair Program 620's heavy leather upholstery and matching ottoman make it a timeless piece of furniture. The boxy seat and high backrest add a sense of stately elegance.

Der schwere Lederbezug und ein passender Hocker machen den Sessel 620 zu einem zeitlosen Möbelstück. Der kastenförmige Sitz und hohe Rückenlehne geben ihm stattliche Eleganz.

Dieter
Rams

Dieter Rams (born in 1932 in Wiesbaden) is a German industrial designer and a prominent figure in the Functionalist design movement. Rams famously characterized his design philosophy as "less is better," and developed ten principles of "good design" which guides his work throughout his career. They include clarity of form, serviceability, environmental sustainability and durability. In 2009, Rams stated that Apple is the only other company currently designing products according to his principles.

After studying architecture and carpentry in Wiesbaden, Rams teamed up with Hans Gugelot to design the "SK-4" record player and radio in1956. The "SK-4" was one of the first consumer products to make use of plexiglass, and was a leading example of functional design in the post-war period. Rams became chief of design at the electronics manufacturer Braun in 1961. He held the position for over 30 years, developing a wide range of household products, from record players to coffee makers and calculators. Many of his products have been shown in museums around the world, including the Museum of Modern Art in New York. In 1995, he started sdr+, his own furniture design company, through which he is able to manufacture his own designs, including Shelving System "606" (designed in 1960) and Armchair "620" (designed in 1962) as well as newer projects.

Dieter Rams (geb. 1932 in Wiesbaden) ist ein deutscher Industriedesigner und ein bekannter Vertreter des funktionellen Designs. Rams studierte Architektur und Innenarchitektur in Wiesbaden, wo er auch eine Tischlerlehre absolvierte.

Rams Beschreibung seiner Design-Philosophie lautet „weniger, aber besser". Er entwickelte außerdem zehn Regeln für gutes Design, auf die er seine Arbeit aufbaut. Diese Regeln beinhalten Unaufdringlichkeit, Brauchbarkeit, Umweltfreundlichkeit und Langlebigkeit. Im Jahr 2009 meinte Rams, dass Apple das einzige andere Unternehmen sei, welches sich ebenfalls an seine Regeln hielt.

1956 entwickelte Rams zusammen mit Hans Gugelot den Plattenspieler und Radio „SK-4". Dieser war eines der ersten Verbraucherprodukte, in welchem Plexiglas verwendet wurde, und ein herausragendes Beispiel des funktionellen Designs der Nachkriegszeit. 1961 wurde Rams Chefdesigner bei dem Elektrogeräte-Hersteller Braun. Er war mehr als 30 Jahre in dieser Position tätig, und entwickelte während dieser Zeit eine große Vielfalt an elektronischen Produkten, von Plattenspielern über Kaffeemaschinen bis hin zu Taschenrechnern. Viele dieser Produkte wurden in Museen in der ganzen Welt gezeigt, unter anderem dem Museum of Modern Art in New York. 1995 gründete er seine eigene Möbeldesign-Firma sdr+, mit der er seine eigenen Entwürfe auch produzieren kann. Zu diesen gehören das Regalsystem „606" (entworfen 1960), der Sessel „620" (entworfen 1962) sowie weitere, neuere Projekte.

Shelving System 606 can be mounted on a wall or left free-standing. Lighter a the top than at the bottom, the shelving system offers plenty of storage options without cramping the space.

Regalsystem 606 kann an der Wand befestigt oder frei im Raum platziert werden. Es ist im oberen Bereich leichter als im unteren und bietet viel Stauraum ohne den Raum einzuengen.

Container Program 980/981 is a sideboard, a
cupboard, and a shelf. The modular elements can
be assembled to suit the needs of any particular
environment.

Das Container Programm 980/981 beinhaltet
ein Sideboard, einen Schrank und ein Regal.
Die Baukastenelemente können passend an die
Bedürfnisse einzelner Umgebungen zusammengesetzt werden.

First designed in 1962, Lounge Chair Program 620's shell is actually made of polyester and fiberglass.

1962 entworfen, ist die Schale des Sesselprogramms 620 aus Polyester und Glasfaser.

Le Bambole, meaning "the dolls", convey comfort and softness from the start. The apparent absence of supporting frame makes the inviting armchair look like a giant, springy cushion.

Le Bambole bedeutet „die Puppen" und suggeriert Weichheit und Komfort von Anfang an. Scheinbar ohne Stützrahmen, erscheint der einladende Sessel wie ein riesiges federndes Kissen.

Mario
Bellini

Mario Bellini (born February 1, 1935) is a world renowned Italian architect and designer. In 1959, he graduated from Polytechnic Institute of Milan with a degree in architecture, and was soon hired as chief design consultant at Olivetti. His career rapidly gained momentum as he extended his talents to urban planning, industrial design and furniture design. By the 1970s and 1980s, he was creating furniture for B&B Italia and Cassina, building the Tokyo Design Center and the Yokohama business park in Japan, and designing a range of hi-fi systems and electronics for Yamaha. In 1987, the Museum of Modern Art in New York held a retrospective exhibition of his work to date, which included, among others, the "Cab chair", created for Cassina in 1977. The comfortable, versatile chair's flexible enameled steel frame and leather skin made it an instant classic. Over the course of his career, Bellini has won eight Compasso d'Oro awards, and in 2004, the Medaglia d'Oro was conferred on him by the President of Italy. His most recent projects include the Milan Convention Center at the Milan Trade Fair, which will be the largest of its kind in Europe.

Mario Bellini (geboren am 1.2.1935) ist ein weltberühmter italienischer Architekt und Designer.

Er schloss sein Architekturstudium im Jahre 1959 am Polytechnikum Mailand ab und wurde bald darauf der leitende Designberater von Olivetti. Seine Karriere kam immer mehr in Bewegung, da er sein Talent auch zur Städteplanung und für industrielles Design und Möbeldesign nutzte. In den 1970er und 80er Jahren entwickelte er Möbel für B&B Italia und Cassina, baute das Tokyo Design Center und das Yokohama Gewerbegebiet in Japan und entwarf eine Reihe von Hi-Fi Systemen und elektronischen Geräten für Yamaha. 1987 organisierte das Museum of Modern Art in New York eine retrospektive Ausstellung seiner Werke bis zu jener Zeit, unter anderem den Stuhl „Cab", den er 1977 für Cassina entworfen hatte. Der komfortable, vielseitige emaillierte Stahlrahmen und der Lederbezug machten diesen Stuhl sofort zu einem Klassiker.

Im Laufe seiner Karriere gewann Bellini acht Mal den Compasso d'Oro und im Jahre 2004 verlieh ihm der italienische Staatspräsident die Medaglia d'Oro. Eines seiner jüngsten Projekte ist das Mailänder Konferenzzentrum auf dem Messegelände von Mailand, welches das größte seiner Art in Europa werden wird.

The Cab Chair was one of Bellini's first hits, and this timeless design is still wildly popular today. The stylish leather "skin" zips over a flexible metal frame, creating smooth lines.

Der Stuhl Cab war einer der ersten durchschlagenden Erfolge von Bellini, dessen zeitloses Design auch heute noch sehr beliebt ist. Die elegante „Lederhaut" überzieht einen Metallrahmen, wodurch die geraden Linien entstehen.

The lightweight Vol au Vent chair is a cozier take on Bellini's classic, sleek chairs. Fully padded, the chair has optional armrests and can be upholstered in a variety of materials.

Der leichte Stuhl Vol au Vent ist eine gemütlichere Version von Bellinis klassisch-eleganten Stühlen. Durchgängig gepolstert, gibt es den Stuhl wahlweise auch mit Armstützen und in einer großen Auswahl von Materialien.

La Basilica, whose name evokes majestic churches, is supported by six or eight wooden pillars. The result is a regal and enduring oak table that commands attention in any room.

La Basilica, deren Name an majestätische Kirchen erinnert, wird von sechs oder acht Holzständern gestützt. Das Resultat ist ein imposanter, robuster Eichentisch, der in jedem Raum die Aufmerksamkeit auf sich zieht.

La Rotonda's unique mortise and joint assembly supports the sculptural three-legged base. The round table top is available in wood or crystal.

La Rotondas einzigartiger Keilzapfenaufbau stützt den skulpturartigen dreibeinigen Unterbau. Die runde Tischplatte ist in Holz oder Glas erhältlich.

The Air bookshelf's thin metal shelves can bear a
surprising amount of weight, making it not only
discreetly stylish, but also highly functional.

Die dünnen Metallböden des Buchregals Air
haben eine erstaunliche Tragkraft, wodurch das
Regal zurückgenommene Materialität mit großer
Funktionalität vereint.

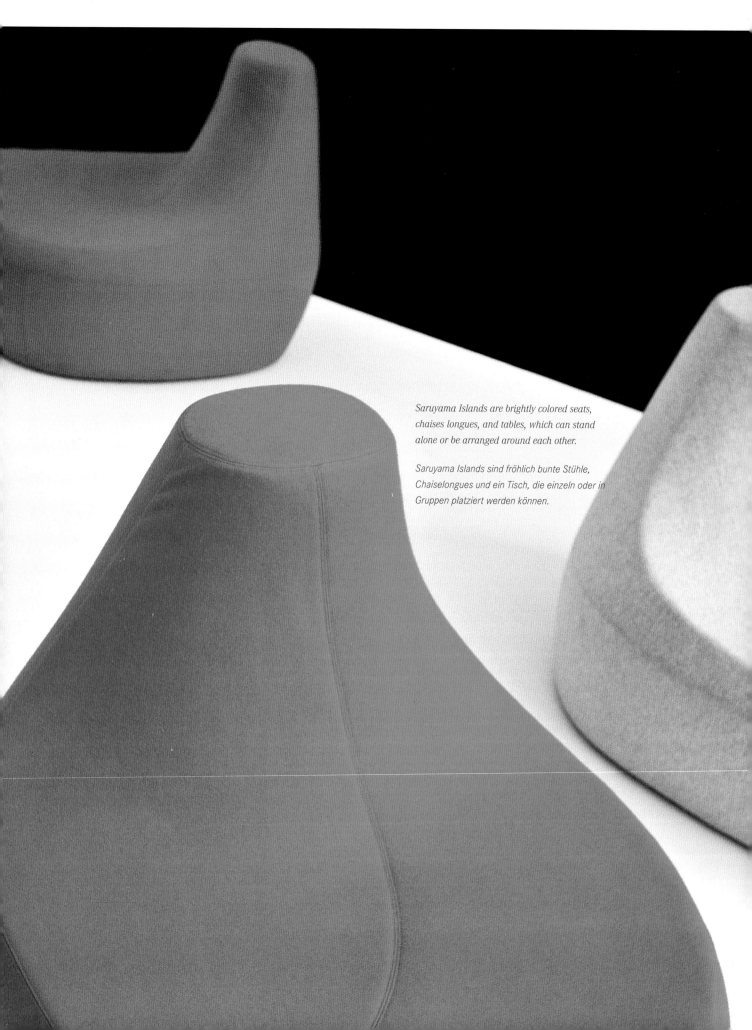

Saruyama Islands are brightly colored seats,
chaises longues, and tables, which can stand
alone or be arranged around each other.

Saruyama Islands sind fröhlich bunte Stühle,
Chaiselongues und ein Tisch, die einzeln oder in
Gruppen platziert werden können.

Toshiyuki
Kita

Toshiyuki Kita (born in 1942 in Osaka) is a Japanese furniture and product designer. He studied industrial design at Naniwa College in Osaka, graduating in 1964, then launched his own design studio in 1967. In 1969, he moved to Milan, where he worked with Mario Bellini, among others, and started another studio. From then on, he moved between Japan and Italy creating furniture, for both European and Asian companies. His first major success was the "Wink" chair, created for Cassina in 1980, a highly original piece which includes a freely movable headrest and exchangeable colored covers. These can be switched around between pieces and washed at home, making the chair easy to personalize. The chair is now featured in the New York Musuem of Modern Art's permanent collection and the Centre Pompidou in Paris. In addition to traditional furniture, he has also worked extensively in consumer electronics, creating massage chairs for Family Inada, and LCD televisions for Sharp. Kita is also very invested in education and in promoting traditional crafts and local industries. He regularly holds seminars and workshops across Europe and Asia.

Toshiyuki Kita (geb. in 1942 in Osaka) ist ein japanischer Möbel- und Produktdesigner. Er studierte am Naniwa College in Osaka bis 1964 Industriedesign und eröffnete dann 1967 sein eigenes Designbüro. 1969 zog er nach Mailand, wo er unter anderem mit Mario Bellini zusammenarbeitete und dort ein weiteres Büro eröffnete. Von diesem Zeitpunkt an pendelte er zwischen Japan und Italien hin und her und entwickelte Möbel für europäische und asiatische Unternehmen. Sein erster berühmter Entwurf war der Sessel „Wink", den er 1980 für Cassina entwickelte.

Das originelle Möbelstück hat eine frei verstellbare Kopfstütze und austauschbare bunte Bezüge. Diese können zwischen einzelnen Sesseln gewechselt und in der Maschine gewaschen werden, womit jeder Sessel eine persönliche Note bekommt. Der Sessel ist Teil der ständigen Sammlung des New York Museum of Modern Art und des Centre Pompidou in Paris. Außer traditionellen Möbeln hat er auch viele Entwürfe im Bereich Verbraucherelektronik erstellt, wie z.B. Massagesessel für Family Inada, und LCD Fernsehgeräte für Sharp. Kita ist auch sehr interessiert am Unterrichten und der Unterstützung von traditionellem Handwerk und Gewerbe. Er veranstaltet regelmäßig Seminare und Workshops in ganz Europa und in Asien.

The fluid, amorphous shapes of the Saruyama Islands make any arrangement possible, and they are little enough to fit well in small spaces.

Die fließenden, amorphen Formen Saruyama Islands ermöglichen alle erdenklichen Zusammenstellungen; außerdem sind sie klein genug, um auch in enge Räume zu passen.

Aki, Biki, and Canta each have their own personalities, but they were all designed as work chairs that could accommodate a range of movement. Canta's armrest can swivel up to become a headrest.

Aki, Biki, und Canta haben jedes seine eigene Persönlichkeit, aber alle wurden als Arbeitsstühle entworfen, die eine Reihe von Bewegungen unterstützen. Cantas Armlehne kann nach oben geklappt werden, um zu einer Kopfstütze zu werden.

Saruyama, which means "Monkey Mountain,"
allows users to sit, lie down, or climb all over it.
The three pieces can be combined to form one
large, round sofa.

Saruyama, was übersetzt „Affenberg" bedeutet,
lässt Nutzer auf ihm sitzen, liegen oder sogar
herumklettern. Die drei Teile können zu einem
einzigen großen runden Sofa zusammengesetzt
werden.

Wink is a playful lounge chair with a many different options. The leg-rest can be extended out from under the seat, the headrests can be moved at will, and the bright covers can be switched around.

Wink ist ein verspielter Klubsessel mit vielen verschiedenen Möglichkeiten. Die Fußstütze kann unter dem Sitz herausgezogen werden, die Kopfstützen können beliebig eingestellt und die bunten Bezüge gewechselt werden.

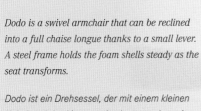

Dodo is a swivel armchair that can be reclined into a full chaise longue thanks to a small lever. A steel frame holds the foam shells steady as the seat transforms.

Dodo ist ein Drehsessel, der mit einem kleinen Hebel zurückgekippt werden kann, so dass eine komplette Chaiselongue entsteht. Ein Stahlrahmen stabilisiert die geschäumten Schalen während der Umwandlung.

MedaPal is an office swivel chair that anticipates the needs the office worker, thanks to its extra flexible backrest with built-in lumbar support, lightweight design, and adjustable armrests.

MedaPal ist ein Bürodrehstuhl der den Bedürf-nissen der Büroarbeit gerecht wird. Er hat eine besonders flexible Rückenlehne mit integrierter Lendenstütze, ein leichtgewichtiges Design und verstellbaren Armlehnen.

Alberto
Meda

Alberto Meda (born in 1945 in Lenno Tremezzina, Italy) was trained as a mechanical engineer at the Polytechnic Institute of Milan. His career began developing plastic laboratory equipment. Starting in 1979, he began working as a freelance industrial designer for a number of companies, including Alias, Vitra and Olivetti. His collaboration with Vitra has lasted more than 20 years and continues to this day, producing a renowned series of chairs and seating systems, including the "MedaPal" office chair. His engineering background, and the pragmatic mindset and attention to detail that come with it, is reflected in his simple, elegant designs and high-tech production techniques.

Since 1983, he has also given lectures in industrial technology and design at universities in Italy and abroad. Some of his work is part of the permanent collections of the Museum of Modern Art in Toyama and New York. He has also received a number of international design awards, including three Compasso d'Oro awards.

Alberto Meda (geboren 1945 in Lenno Tremezzina, Italien) absolvierte eine Ausbildung als Maschinenbauingenieur am Polytechnikum von Mailand. Er begann seine Karriere mit dem Entwickeln von Laborzubehör aus Synthetik. Ab 1979 arbeitete er als freiberuflicher Industriedesigner für eine Reihe von Unternehmen wie Alias, Vitra und Olivetti. Seit 1983 ist er auch Dozent für Industrietechnik und Design an mehreren Universitäten in Italien und in anderen Ländern.

Seine Zusammenarbeit mit Vitra besteht schon seit über 20 Jahren bis heute und während dieser Zeit entwarf er eine berühmte Reihe von Stühlen und Sitzmöbeln, inklusive des Bürostuhls „MedaPal". Der schlichte, elegante Stil seiner Designs und die High-Tech Herstellungsmethoden reflektieren seinen Ingenieurshintergrund und die damit verbundene praktische Denkweise und Liebe zum Detail.

Manche seiner Arbeiten sind Teil der ständigen Sammlung des Museum of Modern Art in Toyama und des Museum of Modern Art in New York. Er erhielt auch eine Reihe von internationalen Designauszeichnungen, wie z.B. drei Compasso d'Oro-Preise.

The original Meda Chair, designed in 1998, also provided great comfort and flexibility with minimal technology. One key feature is very supportive backrest.

Der originale Meda Chair, 1998 entworfen, bietet ebenfalls maximalen Komfort und Flexibilität mit minimaler Technologie. Ein Hauptmerkmal ist seine intensiv stützende Rückenlehne.

Medamorph tables can be round, rectangular, and oblong, and users can adjust the frame to suit different aesthetic or spatial needs.

Medamorph Tische können rund, rechteckig oder länglich sein, wobei die Nutzer den Rahmen verstellen können, um verschiedenen ästhetischen und praktischen Bedürfnissen gerecht zu werden.

The MedaMorph conference table system show-
cases Meda's engineering background. The modular frame consists of four elements that can be
used to build tables of different shapes and sizes.

*Das Konferenztischsystem MedaMorph demons-
triert die Ingenieurerfahrung von Meda. Der
modulare Rahmen besteht aus vier Elementen
aus denen Tische in verschiedenen Formen und
Größen gebaut werden können.*

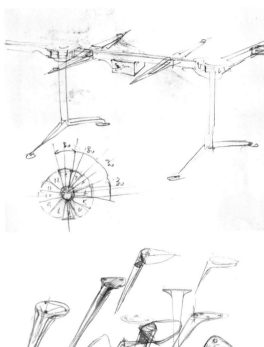

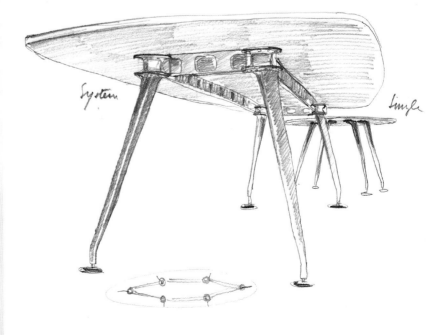

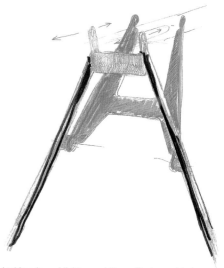

Archimeda's simple, clean design conceals its secret: a special mechanism makes the table height-adjustable, allowing the user to work both sitting or standing.

Archimedas schlichtes und klares Design verbirgt ein Geheimnis: durch einen speziellen Mechanismus kann die Höhe des Tisches verstellt werden, wodurch der Benutzer im Sitzen oder im Stehen arbeiten kann.

Highframe 416 and 417 are a series of stackable chairs with extruded aluminum frames, uphol- stered in leather or in PVC-covered polyester mesh, which has since become a very popular material in deisgn.

Highframe 416 und 417 sind eine Kollektion von stapelbaren Stühlen aus fließgepressten Aluminium-Rahmen, mit Lederpolstern oder PVC– bezogenem Polyesternetz, welches seitdem ein beliebtes Material für die Möbelproduktion ist.

The Catifa 70 Chair combines lightweight design with surprisingly clear form. The curved shell of the seat moves in one, uninterrupted line, and a matching ottoman complements the chair.

Der Catifa Chair 70 ist eine Kombination von leichtgewichtigem Design mit erstaunlich präziser Form. Die gebogene Schale des Sitzes bewegt sich in einer einzigen ununterbrochenen Linie; ein passender Hocker ergänzt den Sessel.

Lievore, Altherr
Molina

Lievore Altherr Molina ist ein Design-Team aus Barcelona, das 1991 von Alberto Lievore (Argentinien), Jeannette Altherr (Deutschland) und Manel Molina (Spanien) gegründet wurde.

Die drei Mitglieder des Teams kombinieren ihre verschiedenen Interessen und Know-How um für diverse Kunden Design, Beratung und künstlerische Gestaltung zu liefern. Eine ihrer längsten Partnerschaften besteht mit der italienischen Design Firma Arper, deren Fokus auf Schlichtheit, Anmut und Transparenz das Designer-Team sofort angesprochen hatte. So ist die „Catifa"-Linie ein Projekt, das in Zusammenarbeit mit Arper entstand. Schlicht und mit technisch hohem Niveau, ohne aufdringlich zu wirken, während sie gleichzeitig eine Balance zwischen Strenge und einem organischen Eindruck finden, veranschaulichen diese Möbel die Design-Philosophie, die beide Teams vereint.

Lievore Altherr Molina is a design team from Barcelona formed in 1991 by Alberto Lievore (Argentina), Jeannette Altherr (Germany) and Manel Molina (Spain). Together, the three members combine their different interests and backgrounds to provide product design, consulting and art direction for a variety of clients. One of their most extended collaborations has been with the Italian design company Arper, whose emphasis on simplicity, grace and transparency of design seemed immediately appealing to the design team. The "Catifa Family" is one project undertaken with Arper. Simple, technologically advanced without being flashy, and achieving a perfect balance between austerity and an organic feel, it exemplifies the design philosophy that brings the two teams together.

Throughout the years the studio has been recognised for its furniture design, as well as its interior design projects, and product and packaging design. In addition to their independent projects, the studio is intensely involved in teaching, giving seminars and classes.

Lievore Altherr Molina has been awarded many national and international awards, including Spain's National Design Award in 1999. Their work has been exhibited in Barcelona, Helsinki, London, Milan, New York, Paris and Tokyo, and they are regularly featured in prestigious design magazines around the world.

Das Studio erhielt von Anfang an große Anerkennung für seine Möbeldesigns, für die Innenarchitektur sowie für Produkt- und Verpackungsentwürfe. Neben seinen Projekten ist das Trio auch stark in der Lehre engagiert und hält eine große Anzahl von Seminaren und Vorlesungen.

Lievore Altherr Molina erhielten viele spanische und internationale Auszeichnungen, wie z. B. den Spanischen National Design Award im Jahr 1999. Ihre Arbeiten wurden in Barcelona, Helsinki, London, Mailand, New York, Paris und Tokio ausgestellt, und erscheinen regelmäßig in führenden Design-Zeitschriften der internationalen Presse.

Catifa is Catalan for "rug", and the other
members of the large series are lightweight chairs
characterized by their thin, curved shells.

Catifa ist katalanisch und bedeutet „Teppich".
Andere Stücke der vielseitigen Reihe sind leichte
Stühle, die durch ihre dünnen, gebogenen Schalen
gekennzeichnet sind.

The Carola chair and armchair are a carefully crafted out of wood, which seem to follow in the legacy of mid-century Scandinavian design.

Stuhl und Sessel Carola sind kunstfertig aus Holz hergestellt und erscheinen als Fortsetzung des legendären skandinavischen Designs der Mitte des letzten Jahrhunderts.

The Duna chairs have a variety of different bases,
including a cantilever frame, a sled base, or
wheels. The molded polyurethane shells mean
that the chairs can also be used outside.

Die Stühle Duna haben eine Vielzahl an verschie-
denen Untergestellen, z.B. einen freischwingenden
Rahmen, ein Schlittenuntergestell oder Rollen.
Durch die Schalen aus gegossenem PU können die
Stühle auch im Freien verwendet werden.

Trenza is an outdoor series, and includes regular chairs as well as a bar stool and a lounge chair. They are all distinguished by their woven seats and lightweight, metal sled frames.

Trenza ist eine Außenmöbel-Kollektion, zu der normale Stühle sowie ein Barhocker und Klubsessel gehören. Alle haben gewebte Sitzflächen und leichte Metall-Schlittenrahmen.

Palm is another series of versatile, lightweight
chairs. The plastic shell is flexible and ergonomi-
cally designed, and the chair comes with a range
of different bases to suit any environment.

Palm ist eine weitere Reihe von vielseitigen leichten Stühlen. Sie haben flexible und ergonomisch
geformte Kunststoffschalen und eine Reihe von
verschiedenen Untergestellen, die zu jedem
Umfeld passen.

Zisa's calm symmetry and repeated shapes were intended to represent the very essence of chair design, with structural clarity and minimalist form being the main features.

Zisas ruhige Symmetrie durch sich wiederholende Formen sollten die wahre Essenz des Stuhldesigns darstellen, wobei klare Strukturen und minimalisti-sche Formen die Hauptmerkmale waren.

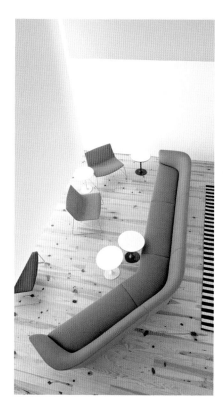

Loop is an elegant but subdued sofa, characterized by soft lines and lightness. The sofa comes
in two-seater and three-seater versions, and the
modules can be combined in larger arrangements.

Loop ist ein elegantes, aber unauffälliges Sofa
mit weichen Konturen und viel Leichtigkeit. Das
Sofa gibt es als Zwei- und Dreisitzer, wobei die
einzelnen Elemente auch zu größeren Ensembles
zusammengefügt werden können.

Saari Armchairs are are stackable and highly
geometric, contrasting rarely-used polygons in the
seat with thin legs set in a strict square shape.

Die Sessel Saari sind sehr leicht stapelbar und
stark geometrisch geformt. Ihre unüblichen Poly-
gone in der Sitzfläche kontrastieren mit dünnen
Beinen, die präzise quadratisch angeordnet sind.

The Team chairs all start out with a basic, supremely lightweight shell, which are then combined with different bases, armrests, and upholstery to create a wide and versatile range.

Die Stühle Team haben alle die gleiche extrem leichte Schale, die mit verschiedenen Unterge- stellen, Armlehnen und Polsterungen kombiniert werden kann, wodurch eine große Vielfalt an Modellen entsteht.

Masai's aesthetic charm comes from the contrast between sharp lines and the inviting upholstery. The seat and back are almost identical rectangles, while the optional armrests are slightly smaller.

Der ästhetische Charme von Masai resultiert aus dem Kontrast von scharf begrenzten Linien und der einladenden Polsterung. Die Sitzfläche und der Rücken sind fast identische Rechtecke, während die wahlweise vorhandenen Armlehnen etwas schmaler sind.

The Solo sofa has a highly comfortable seat
sustained by a die-cast aluminum support. Its size
offers an image of lightness, which is enhanced by
a continuous seat without cushions.

Das Sofa Solo hat eine sehr bequeme Sitzfläche
mit einer druckgegossenen Aluminium-Stütz-
vorrichtung. Durch seine Größe erweckt es den
Eindruck von Leichtigkeit, der noch von der durch-
gängigen Sitzfläche ohne Kissen verstärkt wird.

Antonio
Citterio

Antonio Citterio (born in 1950 in Meda) is an Italian furniture designer and industrial designer, currently working in Milan. He graduated from the Polytechnic Institute of Milan with a degree in architecture, but was only 18 when he designed his first sofa, which won a prize and immediately went into production. In 1972, he opened his own studio for architecture and interior design, and has been working for leading design companies, including Vitra, B&B Italia, and Maxalto, a B&B Italia brand which he directs, ever since. In 1999, he opened Antonio Citterio Patricia Viel and Partners, a multidisciplinary practice which also produces industrial design and graphics.

A prodigiously versatile designer, he has created everything from doorknobs to sofas, lamps, and bathroom fixtures. His pragmatic and timeless designs have won him much international acclaim, and he received the coveted Italian Compasso d'Oro prize for design in 1979 and 1987. He has created interiors for a number of stores around the world. In 2007, he became a member of the Italian Design Council.

Antonio Citterio (geboren 1950 in Meda) ist ein italienischer Möbel- und Industrie-Designer, der in Mailand tätig ist. Er absolvierte ein Architekturstudium am Polytechnikum von Mailand.

Mit nur 18 Jahren entwarf er sein erstes Sofa, das einen Preis gewann und sofort in die Produktion übernommen wurde. 1972 eröffnete er sein eigenes Architektur- und Innenarchitekturstudio, in dem er seit dieser Zeit mit führenden Designfirmen wie Vitra, B&B Italia, und Maxalto, einer B&B Italia-Marke, die er leitet, zusammenarbeitet. Im Jahr 1999 eröffnete er das fachübergreifende Studio Antonio Citterio Patricia Viel and Partners, das auch Industrie- und Grafik-Design anbietet.

Als ungeheuer versatiler Designer entwarf er alle Arten von Dingen, von Türgriffen bis Sofas, Lampen und Badezimmer-Armaturen, sowie die Innenausstattung für eine Reihe von Läden rund um den Globus.

Seine praktischen und zeitlosen Ideen wurden international hoch anerkannt und er erhielt 1979 und 1987 den begehrten italienischen Compasso d'Oro Design-Preis. Im Jahre 2007 wurde er Mitglied des Italian Design Council.

The Charles system meets the requirements of consumers increasingly looking for larger models. The terminal units and the chaise lounge together with a linear element add to the new design variation.

Das System Charles entspricht den Wünschen von Verbrauchern, die immer größere Modelle verlangen. Die Endstücke sowie die Chaiselongue beleben zusammen mit einem linearen Modul die neue Design-Variante.

The Ray sofa's main feature is the U-shaped foot in diecast bronzed nickel aluminum that, along with the seat cushions, contributes to creating an image of a low sofa.

Das Hauptelement des Sofas Ray ist seine U-förmige Basis aus druckgegossenem Nickel-Aluminium, das im Zusammenspiel mit den Sitzkissen den Eindruck eines niedrigen Sofas ergibt.

The Flat.C system, the bookcase, also equipped
to hold the TV set and video/HI-FI accessories as
well, offers a broad range of combination and
color options.

*Das System Flat.C, welches auch Fernseher sowie
Video/HI-FI Geräte aufnehmen kann, bietet eine
große Palette an Kombinationsmöglichkeiten und
Farben.*

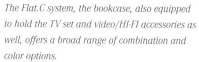

The Suita sofa system is ideally suited to creating flexible arrangements that can be adapted to customer requirements and to fit the available space.

Das Sofasystem Suita ist perfekt geeignet für flexible Gestaltungsmöglichkeiten, die auf die Bedürfnisse der Verbraucher und den vorhandenen Platz zugeschnitten sind.

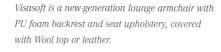

Visasoft is a new-generation lounge armchair with PU foam backrest and seat upholstery, covered with Wool top or leather.

Visasoft ist ein moderner Sessel mit einem Rückenteil aus PU-Schaum und einer Sitzfläche, die mit Wolle oder Leder bezogen sind.

Visavis is a chrome steel, stackable chair with structural clarity and comfort.

Visavis ist ein stapelbarer Stuhl aus Chromstahl, der strukturelle Klarheit und Komfort bietet.

Spatio, a product line for the executive office and conference spaces. Fine wood finishes and carefully crafted aluminum components create a feeling of understated luxury.

Spatio ist eine Produktreihe von Möbeln für Chefetagen und Konferenzräume. Edles Holz und sehr sorgfältig verarbeitete Aluminiumelemente schaffen ein Gefühl von unaufdringlichem Luxus.

The ID Chair Concept brings a subtle, elegant design and light color tones to office spaces and it is also an invaluable help when it comes to maintenance and service.

Das ID Chair Concept vermittelt in Büroräumen ein raffiniertes, elegantes Design und setzt Farbakzente in Kombination mit leichter Pflege.

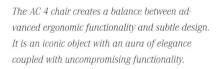

The AC 4 chair creates a balance between advanced ergonomic functionality and subtle design. It is an iconic object with an aura of elegance coupled with uncompromising functionality.

Der Stuhl AC 4 kombiniert hochmoderne ergonomische Funktionalität mit unauffälligem Design. Er ist ein Kultobjekt mit einer Aura von Eleganz im Zusammenspiel mit kompromissloser Funktionalität.

Careful attention to ergonomic design makes the Jean Sofa elegant in line and in comfort.

Das sorgfältig entwickelte ergonomische Design verleiht dem Sofa Jean elegante Linien und erweckt ein Gefühl von Behaglichkeit.

Seats available in three depths distinguish the Harry armchairs, sofas and modular elements, all with classic aluminum feet.

Die Sessel, Sofas und Module der Reihe Harry zeichnen sich durch drei verschiedene Tiefen aus und haben alle klassische Aluminiumbeine.

Ron
Arad

Ron Arad (born 1951 in Tel Aviv) is an Is-raeli architect and industrial designer cur-rently working in London. He studied first at the Bezalel Academy of Art and Design in Jerusalem, and then moved to England to attend the Architectural Association in London, graduating in 1979. His first series of furniture, designed in the early 1980s, often incorporated found objects and scrap metal, which he learned to weld. The imposing "Big Easy" chair, created in 1988, is made from solid sheets of steel that were bent and welded together to cre-ate the chair's voluminous form. Arad later extended his singular aesthetic to differ-ent materials. The "Victoria and Albert" sofas retain a similar sculptural feel and generous proportions, but they are made of more forgiving, synthetic materials, and are available in a range of bright colors. Arad's unique approach to furniture design has earned him great success, and his de-sign work has been exhibited in galleries and museums around the world. He is also an established architect, designing the Tel Aviv Opera and the Design Museum Holon in Israel, as well as several restaurants and stores in Europe.

Ron Arad (geb. 1951 in Tel Aviv) ist ein isra-elischer Architekt und Industriedesigner, der in London tätig ist. Er studierte zunächst an der Kunstakademie in Jerusalem, wonach er 1973 nach London an die Architectural As-sociation School of Architecture ging und dort sein Studium 1979 beendete.

Seine erste Möbelserie, die er Anfang der 1980er Jahre entwarf, enthielt oft Fund-sachen und Altmetall, das er zu schweißen lernte. Der beeindruckende Sessel „Big Easy", 1988 entworfen, besteht aus massi-ven Stahlplatten, die gebogen und zusam-mengeschweißt wurden, um die gewaltige Form des Sessels zu ergeben. Arad erwei-terte seine einzigartige Ästhetik später auf andere Materialien. Die Sofas „Victoria und Albert" haben den gleichen bildhauerischen Eindruck und großzügige Proportionen, sind aber aus nachgiebigerem synthetischem Material in einer Reihe von bunten Farben gefertigt. Arad ist sehr erfolgreich mit seinen einzigartigen Möbeldesigns und seine Arbei-ten wurden in Galerien und Museen rund um die Welt ausgestellt. Er ist außerdem ein eta-blierter Architekt, der Gebäude wie die Tel Aviv Oper und das Design Museum Holon in Israel sowie viele europäische Restaurants und Läden entwarf.

The Victoria and Albert Collection includes two armchairs and one imposing sofa. Their pillowy shapes and bright colors exude comfort and optimism. Little Albert can be also be used outdoors.

Zu der Kollektion Victoria and Albert gehören zwei Sessel und ein beeindruckendes Sofa. Die weichen Formen und leuchtenden Farben strahlen Komfort und Optimismus aus. Little Albert kann auch im Freien verwendet werden.

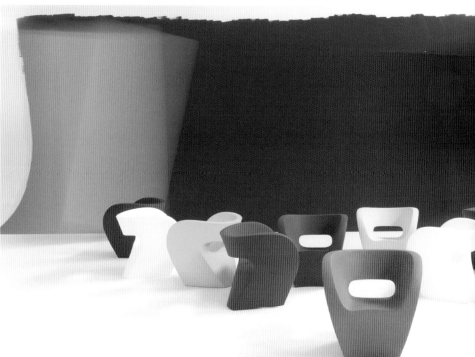

The Victoria and Albert Sofa's expansive curves dominate the series. Using moulded resin, steel supports and polyurethane foam, Arad combines cutting-edge technology with pure imagination.

Die ausladenden Kurven des Victoria and Albert-Sofas bestimmen die Kollektion. Durch die Verwendung von gegossenem Kunstharz, von Stahlstützen und PU-Schaum verbindet Arad modernste Technologie mit einzigartiger Vorstellungskraft.

Tom Vac chair is cast out of one continuous plastic shell. The wide frame makes it especially comfortable, and it is just as suitable for an office as it is for an outdoor party.

Der Stuhl Tom Vac ist aus einer durchgehenden Plastikschale geformt. Durch den breiten Rahmen ist er besonders gemütlich und sowohl für ein Büro als auch für eine Party im Freien geeignet.

The Do-Lo-Rez Sofa is made up of foam units of various shapes and colors, which are arranged into a surprising seating system. Steel pins provide stability, while the blocks seem to float freely above.

Das Sofa Do-Lo-Rez besteht aus Schaumstoffelementen in verschiedenen Formen und Farben, die ein überraschendes Sitzmöbelsystem ergeben. Stahlbolzen liefern die benötigte Stabilität, während die Blöcke scheinbar frei darüber schweben.

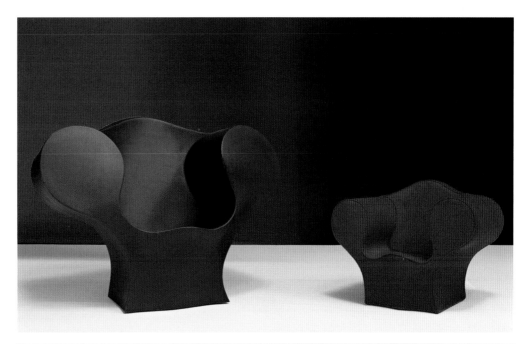

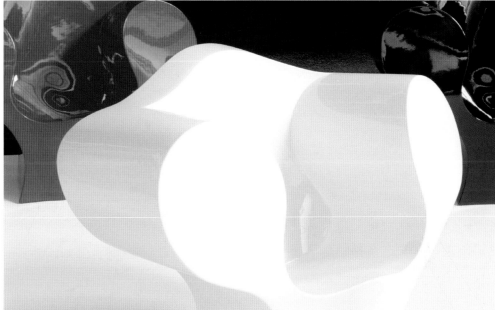

The Spring Collection is a softer take on Arad's famous Big Easy, which is made of welded sheet metal. Soft Big Easy, made of polyurethane foam, retains a sculptural feel without sacrificing comfort.

Die Spring Collection ist eine weichere Variante von Arad's berühmten Big Easy, der aus geschweißtem Stahlblech besteht. Der Soft Big Easy aus PU-Schaum erweckt auch heute noch den Eindruck einer Skulptur in Kombination mit ausgesprochen komfortablem Sitzen.

*The Favela armchair is named after the the shan-
tytowns in Brazil which inspired its construction.
It is made from many pieces of natural wood,
glued and nailed together by hand.*

*Der Sessel Favela ist nach den informellen Sied-
lungen in Brasilien benannt. Er besteht aus vielen
Naturholzteilen, die von Hand zusammengeklebt
und genagelt sind.*

Fernando & Humberto
Campana

Fernando and Humberto Campana (born in 1953 and 1961, respectively, in São Paulo) are currently Brazil's most famous design team. Humberto was formerly a lawyer, and Fernando is a trained architect. After their first breakthrough in 1998, with the "Vermelha" chair series, the Campana brothers have continued to make a name for themselves with their creative and innovative designs. One theme that re-occurs throughout their work is the recycling or re-purposing of found objects, with surprising results. Whether converting objects of no value into high-quality products or simply finding new uses in unexpected textures and materials, this combination of chance encounters with skillful craftsmanship has brought them international success. The "Favela Chair" was put together out of scraps of wood found in

the slums of São Paulo, while the "Sushi Chair" was fashioned out of rolled up strips of various colorful materials. They are not afraid to mix textures either, as proved by the "Cipria Attila" sofa, which is half faux fur and half shiny, colorful leather. Unlike most other designers today, the Campana brothers do not work with computers during the design process. Instead, since they often draw their inspiration from the materials themselves, the design process begins organically, in the studio.

The Campanas have been featured in the Museum of Modern Art in New York and at the Centre Pompidou in Paris.

Fernando und Humberto Campana (geboren 1953 und1961 in São Paulo) sind derzeit Brasiliens bekanntestes Designerteam. Humberto arbeitete zuvor als Rechtsanwalt, während Fernando ein ausgebildeter Architekt ist.

Nach ihrem ersten Durchbruch im Jahr 1998 mit der Stuhlserie „Vermelha" festigten die Campana-Brüder ihren Ruf durch eine Reihe von kreativen und innovativen Entwürfen. Ein häufiges Motiv ihrer Arbeiten ist dabei die Wiederverwendung oder Umwertung von Fundsachen mit verblüffenden Resultaten. Ob es sich um die Umwandlung von wertlosen Dingen in hochwertige Produkte handelt oder um das Entdecken neuer Verwendungen von unerwarteten Strukturen und Materialien, die Kombination von zufälligen Dingen mit höchster Kunstfertigkeit hat ihnen internationalen Ruhm beschert. So wurde der Stuhl „Favela" aus Holzresten aus den Slums von São Paulo zusammengefügt, während der Stuhl „Sushi" aus gerollten Streifen von verschiedenen bunten Materialien fabriziert wurde. Sie scheuten sich auch nicht davor, verschiedene Strukturen zu mischen wie bei dem Sofa „Cipria Attila", welches zur einen Hälfte aus Kunstfell und zur anderen aus glänzend buntem Leder besteht. Anders als die meisten Designer heutzutage arbeiten die Campana-Brüder nicht mit Computern. Stattdessen lassen sie sich oft von den Materialien selbst inspirieren, so dass der Designprozess organisch im Studio beginnt.

Arbeiten der Campanas befinden sich im Museum of Modern Art in New York und dem Centre Pompidou in Paris.

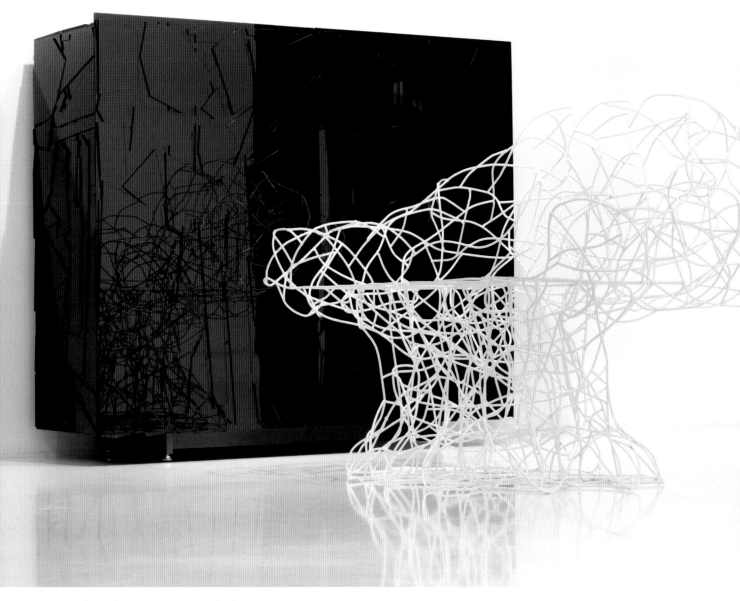

The Corallo frameless armchair is made of an irregular weave of stainless steel wire. A coat of epoxy paint finish in coral, white or black color protects the steel.

Der rahmenlose Sessel Corallo besteht aus ungleichmäßig geflochtenem, rostfreiem Stahldraht. Eine Epoxidlack-Schicht in korallenrot, weiß oder schwarz schützt den Stahl.

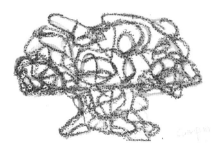

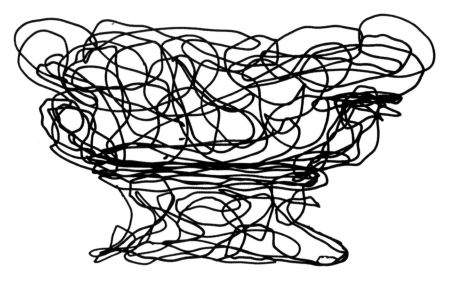

Sushi is a multicolored seat is made by rolling up fabrics and materials of different types and thicknesses and then squeezing them into a large, flexible polyurethane and fabric tube.

Sushi ist ein mehrfarbiger Stuhl, der hergestellt wird, indem Stoffe und Materialien verschiedener Arten und Stärken in eine große flexible PU- und Stoffröhre gepresst werden.

Leatherworks's imperfect and ragged exterior conceals outstanding craftsmanship of assembly, stitching, and trimming.

Hinter dem zerklüfteten und unvollkommenen Äußeren von Leatherworks verbirgt sich seine kunstvolle Zusammenfügung durch Nähte und Besätze.

The Azul armchair is hand-made in a skillful sequence, weaving 650 meters of special rope with an acrylic core covered in cotton. Its metal frame is coated with epoxy powders.

Der Sessel Azul ist handgemacht, indem 650 Meter eines Spezialseils mit einem Acryl-Inneren und Baumwolle-Äußeren verwebt werden. Sein Metallrahmen ist mit Epoxidpuder beschichtet.

The Jenette chairs are made with injection-moulded polyurethane. Its stainless steel slab backrest is hidden behind a curtain of approximately 900 flexible stalks of PVC.

Die Stühle Jenette sind aus Spritzguss-PU hergestellt. Ihre Rückenlehnen aus Edelstahl sind hinter einem Vorhang verborgen, der aus ungefähr 900 flexiblen PVC-Stäben besteht.

The Brasilia tables are a chaotic mosaic of reflex pieces. The brilliant colors pay tribute to the designers' country of origin and the stones on which the capital, Brasilia, was built.

Die Tische Brasilia sind aus einem chaotischen Mosaik von reflektierenden Glasstückchen zusammengesetzt. Die leuchtenden Farben sind ein Tribut an das Heimatland des Designers und die Steine, auf welchen die Hauptstadt Brasilia gebaut ist.

The Cabana is a storage unit arranged around a central column supporting five shelves: the structure, in aluminum and other metals, is entirely concealed by dangling lengths of fireproofed raffia.

Cabana ist ein Aufbewahrungsmöbel, das um eine zentrale Säule angeordnet ist, welche fünf Regalböden trägt. Das Gebilde, welches in Aluminium und anderen Metallen ausgeführt ist, wird komplett durch herabhängende Streifen aus feuerfestem Raphiabast verborgen.

This iconic settee, Cipria Attila, has nine cushions
fixed to an invisible metal tube frame. Two cushions are encased in gold leather and the other
seven are lined with natural and brown eco-fur.

Das Kultsofa Cipria Attila besteht aus neun Kissen,
die an einem unsichtbaren Stahlrohr-Rahmen
angebracht sind. Zwei Kissen sind in Goldleder
eingehüllt, während die anderen mit naturfarbe-
nem und braunem Öko-Fell bezogen sind.

Cotto is a table with a stainless steel structure and
legs, and thick aluminum top. The tabletop is set
with eight large, variously shaped and textured
pieces of treated terracotta.

Cotto ist ein Tisch mit einer rostfreien Stahlstruk-
tur und Beinen mit einer dicken Aluminiumplatte.
Die Tischplatte ist mit acht großen, verschieden
geformten und strukturierten Stücken aus behan-
deltem Terrakotta bedeckt.

The design on the rigid yet soft Jensen armchair is highlighted by a visible zipper around the external structure, which is perched on a molded, die-cast aluminum base.

Das Design des festen, aber gleichzeitig weichen Sessels Jensen ist unterstrichen von einem sicht-baren Reißverschluss ringsum die äußere Struktur, die auf einem ausgeformten druckgegossenen Aluminium-Fußgestell sitzt.

Rodolfo
Dordoni

Rodolfo Dordoni (born in 1954 in Milan) is an Italian architect and designer. In 1979, he graduated from the Polytechnic Institute of Milan with a degree in architecture, and then went on to become the art director for Cassina until 1989. He specialized in image strategy, branding, and communication as well as product design, but maintained an independent career in furniture design alongside his work at Cassina. His design process reflects his wide range of expertise, and includes everything from the initial conception of each piece to the appropriate marketing strategy. His furniture pieces distinguish themselves through creative, innovative details supported by an elegant clarity of form. The "Boboli" table surprises the viewer with its dynamic base, which is composed of iron plates and extruded aluminum slats. The metal contrasts sharply with the crystal tabletop, but the form remains subdued and classic. His most recent projects include interior design of both residential and commercial spaces, including shops, restaurants, boats, and hotels.

Rodolfo Dordoni (geb. 1954 in Mailand) ist ein italienischer Architekt und Designer. 1979 schloss er sein Architekturstudium am Polytechnikum in Mailand ab und arbeitete danach bis 1989 als Art Director für Cassina. Dort war er Spezialist für Image Strategie, Markenbildung, Kommunikation und Produktdesign, hat aber gleichzeitig neben seiner Arbeit für Cassina eine unabhängige Karriere als Möbeldesigner gemacht.

Sein Designprozess spiegelt seine weitreichende Erfahrung und sein Know-How wider; es besteht aus dem kompletten Ablauf von der ersten Idee für jedes Stück bis zur passenden Marketingstrategie. Seine Möbelstücke zeichnen sich durch kreative, innovative Details – unterstützt durch eine elegante, klare Formensprache – aus. Der Tisch „Boboli" überrascht mit seinem dynamischen Untergestell aus Eisenplatten und Aluminium-Strangpressprofilen. Das Metall steht in starkem Kontrast zu der Tischplatte aus Kristall, während die Form zurückhaltend klassisch bleibt. Zu seinen jüngsten Projekten gehört die Innenausstattung von Wohn- und Geschäftsräumen, unter anderem Läden, Restaurants, Boote und Hotels.

The molded aluminum die-cast feet characterize the Allen sofa by elevating it from the floor, and soft lines and rounded shapes are achieved with the unique arm detailing.

Die ausgeformten druckgegossenen Aluminium-Füße charakterisieren das Sofa Allen, indem sie es vom Boden abheben, während sanfte Linien und runde Formen durch die einzigartige Armlehnen-konstruktion entstehen.

Martin is an extremely comfortable armchair, fitted with a metal base. To increase comfort, the frame accommodates a goose down quilt which results in enhanced softness.

Martin ist ein extrem bequemer Sessel mit einem Metallfußgestell. Für zusätzlichen Komfort sorgt innerhalb des Rahmens eine Gänsedaunen-Steppdecke, die die Weichheit noch verstärkt.

The Hamilton sofa system is made of independent seating "islands" which can be positioned around the room to create a variety of different seating arrangements.

Das Sofa-System Hamilton besteht aus einzelnen Sitzinseln, die im Raum verteilt werden können, um verschiedene Sitzgelegenheiten zu gestalten.

The Blake chair is a classic design whose suspension is provided by woven elastic strips with high rubber content and its padding is provided from fireproof polyurethane foam.

Der Stuhl Blake ist ein klassisches Design, dessen Federung aus gewobenen, elastischen Streifen mit hohem Gummigehalt besteht, während seine Polsterung aus feuerfestem PU-Schaum ist.

The Pilotta armchair is the first design work for
Cassina, an extraordinary lightness and construc-
tional know-how, authentic structural cabinet-
making joinery and taut leather surfaces.

Der Sessel Pilotta war Dordonis erste Designarbeit
für Cassina. Er verbindet außergewöhnliche Leichtigkeit und Kunstfertigkeit mit solider struktureller
Schreinerarbeit und straffen Lederoberflächen.

The Van Dyck table is fitted with a peculiar metal base, made up of three tubular legs crossed with each other. It boasts surfaces varying in shape: round, rectangular and square.

Der Tisch Van Dyck hat ein ungewöhnliches Metallfußgestell aus drei gekreuzten Röhrenbeinen. Zur Auswahl stehen drei verschiedene Tischplatten: rund, rechteckig und quadratisch.

Light and yet "solid" and reassuring Eloro sofa reappropriates the extraordinary legacy of experience, knowledge and skills in manufacturing with timber.

Leicht und trotzdem „massiv" und beruhigend, verkörpert das Sofa Eloro das außergewöhnliche Erbe von Erfahrung, Wissen und Können in der Holzverarbeitung.

The Boboli table is composed of a dark tempered crystal tabletop which rest on top extruded aluminum slats. These are available in white or black lacquer finish or polished chrome.

Der Tisch Boboli besteht aus einer dunklen Hartglas-Kristalltischplatte, die auf stranggepressten Aluminiumplatten ruht. Diese gibt es sowohl schwarz als auch weiß lackiert und aus poliertem Chrom.

Sled recalls the American interior design of the '60s. This low, lean and sleek sofa is ideal for both public areas and domestic settings.

Sled erinnert an den amerikanischen Stil der 1960er Jahre. Dieses niedrige, schlanke und ranke Sofa passt ideal in öffentliche und private Räume.

The Déjà-vu Chair is borderline sculptural art. Its clean polished aluminum structure can be complemented with optional wood veneer on the reverse of the backrest.

Der Stuhl Déjà-vu ist fast Bildhauerkunst. Seine saubere Struktur aus poliertem Aluminium kann wahlweise mit Holzfurnier auf der Rückseite der Rückenlehne ergänzt werden.

Naoto
Fukasawa

Naoto Fukasawa (born in 1956) is a Japanese industrial designer and furniture designer. He graduated from Tama Art University in 1980, and then started working at Seiko Epson, where he adapted micro-technology developed from wristwatch technology to design wrist TVs and mini printers. In 1989, he moved to the United States, where he worked for a number of technology companies, including Apple. Upon his return to Japan, he began holding design workshops, which led to his design for a wall-mounted CD player, which is now distributed worldwide by Muji and is featured in the New York Museum of Modern Art's permanent collection. Fukusawa characterizes his approach to design as "without thought": instead of over- analyzing form and function, he is more interested in an instinctual feel for the object he is creating, and designs with the human unconsciousness in mind. The "Papillo" chair for example, designed for B&B Italia in 2010, was meant to look totally and obviously comfortable, so Fukusawa looked for a shape that could be read as the very shape of "relaxation" itself. The result is an armchair that looks like a big, soft toy, but retains the same understated elegance that make all of Fukusawa's designs stand out.

Naoto Fukasawa (geb. 1956) ist ein japanischer Industrie- und Möbeldesigner. Er studierte an der Tama Art University bis zu seinem Abschluss 1980 und arbeitete dann für Seiko Epson, wo er die Mikrotechnologie der Armbanduhren zum Entwickeln von Armbandfernsehgeräten und Minidruckern verwendete. 1989 ließ er sich in den USA nieder, wo er für eine Reihe von Technologieunternehmen, unter anderem Apple, arbeitete. Nach seiner Rückkehr nach Japan veranstaltete er Design-Workshops, die zu seinem Entwurf eines Wand-CD-Spielers führten, der heutzutage weltweit von Muji vertrieben wird und der in der ständigen Sammlung des New York Museum of Modern Art zu sehen ist. Fukusawa charakterisiert seinen Designansatz als „gedankenlos": Anstatt Form und Funktion übermäßig zu analysieren, ist er eher an dem instinktiven Gefühl für das Objekt, das er erschafft interessiert und entwirft so Dinge, bei dem er das menschliche Unterbewusstsein im Sinn hat. Der Sessel „Papillo" zum Beispiel, 2010 entworfen für B&B Italia, sollte absolut und direkt komfortabel erscheinen. Fukusawa suchte nach einer Form, die als die wahre Essenz der „Entspannung als solche" interpretiert werden konnte. Das Resultat ist ein Sessel, der wie ein großes weiches Spielzeug erscheint und trotzdem die gleiche unaufdringliche Eleganz ausstrahlt wie alle anderen Designs von Fukusawa.

The Déjà-vu Family also includes the aluminum Déjà-Vu Stool, whose legs come in three different heights.

Zu der Déjà-vu Reihe gehört auch ein Hocker, der in drei verschiedenen Beinlängen erhältlich ist.

The Déjà-vu Console Table has a foldable top not on the length but on the width allowing a multiple use, and the standard Déjà-vu Table has a large oval top with a wooden finish.

Die Platte des Konsoltischs Déjà-vu ist nicht der Länge sondern der Breite nach gefaltet was ihn sehr vielfältig macht, während der Standard Tisch eine große ovale Tischplatte in Holzausführung hat.

The fluid design of the Papilio armchairs is carved out of the trunk of an upside-down cone, providing a roomy upper part. They can swivel 360°.

Die fließende Form der Papilio Sessel weitet sich nach oben, wodurch ein großzügiger oberer Teil entsteht. Sie können sich um 360° drehen.

Shelf X is a bookcase produced in a limited edition of 300 pieces. It is marked by an X diagonal, making the perimeter and the shelves part of the bearing structure.

Shelf X ist ein Bücherregal das in begrenzter Auflage von 300 Stück produziert wurde. Es zeichnet sich durch ein strukturelles diagonales X aus, wodurch der Umfang und die Regale in die Tragestruktur mit einbezogen werden.

Cloud has gently curved edges and a tubular steel
base. The curves strengthen the seating surface,
spanning up to three meters without additional
support in the center of the sofa.

Cloud hat sanft gerundete Kanten und ein Stahl-
rohruntergestell. Die Kurven stützen die Sitzober-
fläche und überbrücken bis zu drei Metern ohne
zusätzlichen Halt in der Mitte des Sofas.

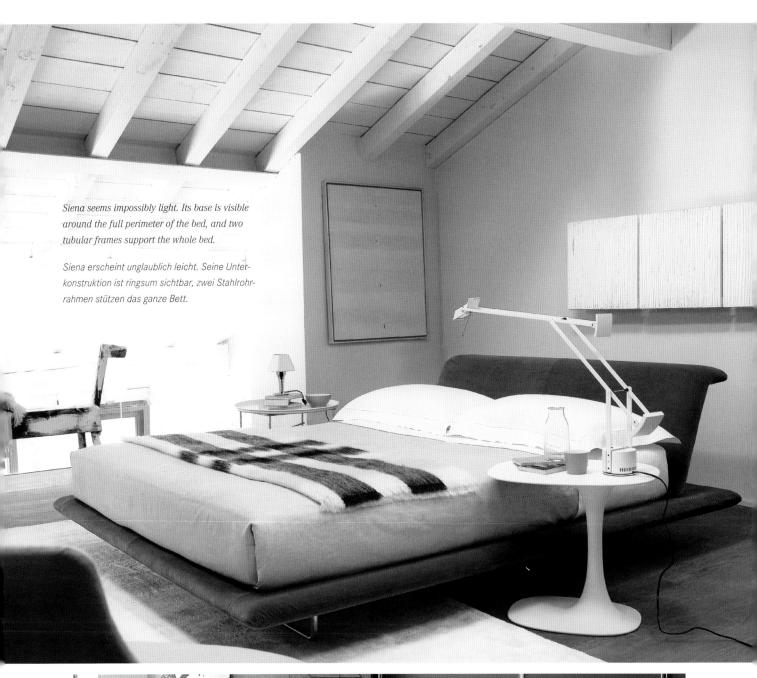

Siena seems impossibly light. Its base is visible around the full perimeter of the bed, and two tubular frames support the whole bed.

Siena erscheint unglaublich leicht. Seine Unter-konstruktion ist ringsum sichtbar, zwei Stahlrohr-rahmen stützen das ganze Bett.

Log includes benches in two sizes, a storage table and a log stool or chair. It is crafted from oak with natural clear lacquer finish and it is completely hollow.

Zur Log Serie gehören zwei Bänke in zwei Größen, sowie ein Aufbewahrungstisch und ein Hocker oder Stuhl. Alle werden aus Eiche mit naturfarbenen Lackoberflächen hergestellt und sind gänzlich hohl.

The Titikaka bench uses thin slats of wood that curve around the aluminum frame, lending the seat an ergonomic style.

Für die Bank Titikaka wurden dünne Holzlatten verwendet die sich um den Aluminiumrahmen winden wodurch der Sitz einen ergonomischen Anstrich bekommt.

The Shelving System is based on Alvar Aalto's
L-system. The modular shelving unit features
lacquered birch ladders and painted shelves.

Das Regalsystem basiert auf Alvar Aaltos
L-System. Die Elemente im Baukastenprinzip be-
stehen aus klar lackierten Birkenstützen und farbig
lackierten Böden.

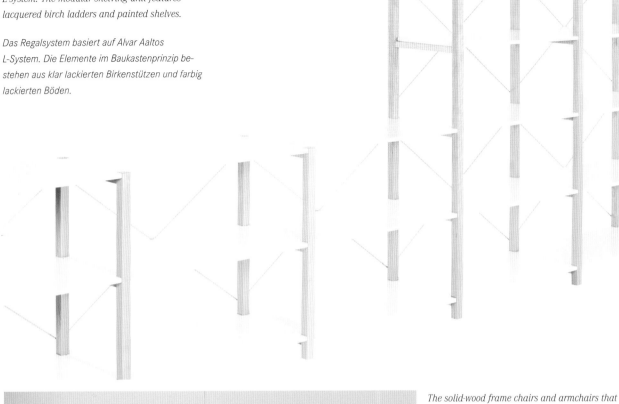

The solid-wood frame chairs and armchairs that
make up the 130 series have padded seats, in a
range of bold color options for the upholstered
elements.

Die Massivholz-Stühle mit oder ohne Armlehne der
Serie 130 haben gepolsterte Sitzflächen in einer
Reihe von leuchtenden Farben.

Wall Sofa's solid wooden frame and repeating rectangular shapes are reassuringly solid.

Der massive Holzrahmen des Sofas Wall und seine wiederholte rechteckige Form haben eine beruhigend solide Ausstrahlung.

Piero
Lissoni

Piero Lissoni (geboren 1956 in Seregno) ist ein italienischer Architekt und Designer. Er studierte Architektur am Polytechnikum von Mailand. Nachdem er als Designer und Art Director für Möbelhersteller wie Living Divani und Porro tätig war, eröffnete er 1986 sein eigenes Studio, Lissoni Associati. Zur Bandbreite seiner Arbeiten gehören Architektur, Innenarchitektur, Möbel- und Industriedesign und sogar Grafik und Werbung. Seine schlichten, aber vielseitigen Möbel sind sehr beliebt.

Seine Design-Philosophie distanziert sich von dem Funktionalismus, der während des größten Teils des 20. Jahrhunderts vorherrschend war, und versucht stattdessen die gesamten menschlichen Aktivitäten und Bedürfnisse anzusprechen. Das Ablagesystem „Radar", entworfen für Cassina, ist ein kreatives Spiel mit Volumen, das neue, fast schon abstrakte Konfigurationen ermöglicht, während die Tische „Mex cube", ebenfalls für Cassina, beliebig zusammengestellt werden können, um verschiedene Oberflächen für verschiedene Nutzungen zu bieten. Zu seinen jüngsten Projekten gehört die Innenausstattung des David Citadel Hotel in Jerusalem und einer Reihe privater Villen in ganz Europa.

Piero Lissoni (born in 1956 in Seregno) is an Italian architect and designer. He studied architecture at the Polytechnic Institute of Milan, and after working as designer and art director for furniture manufacturers like Living Divani and Porro, he opened his own studio, Lissoni Associati, in 1986.

Since then, his range of work has included architecture, interior design, furniture and industrial design, and even graphic design and advertising. His simple but versatile furniture design has earned him great acclaim. His design philosophy moves away from the functionalism that defined much of the 20th century, and instead seeks to accommodate human beings in their whole range of activities and needs. The "Radar" storage unit, created for Cassina, is a creative play on volumes that allows for a new, almost abstract arrangement of storage space, and the "Mex cube" tables, also for Cassina, can be grouped at will, creating different surface configurations for different uses. His current projects include interior design for the David Citadel Hotel in Jerusalem, and a number of private villas throughout Europe.

Extrasoft is a modular sofa system made up of thick, rectangular elements that can be arranged at will. These have wooden structures and polyurethane and goose-down padding.

Extrasoft ist ein modulares Sofasystem, das aus dicken rechteckigen Elementen besteht, die nach Wunsch zusammengesetzt werden können. Sie haben Holzstrukturen mit einer Polsterung aus Polyurethan und Gänsedaunen.

Île's slender metal frame supports a thin seat, from which taller and bigger armrest and back-rests build up. This minimizes the base, and make the heavier parts seem to float above it.

Der schlanke Metallrahmen von Île stützt einen schmalen Sitz aus dem sich die längeren und breiteren Armlehne und Rücken ergeben. Dadurch wird das Untergestell minimiert und schwereren Teile erscheinen als darüber schwebend.

Moov is a dynamic sofa design, lifted off the ground with a steel frame, but solidly anchored in space thanks to its wide armrests and broad back.

Moov ist ein dynamisches Sofadesign, dass durch einen Stahlrahmen vom Boden angehoben wird aber auf Grund seiner breiten Armlehnen und ausladendem Rücken fest im Raum verankert ist.

Eve is a small armchair that comes either in metal or wood, with leather upholstery. The different materials bring out different sides of the minimal frame, from simple warmth to strict geometry.

Eve ist ein kleiner Sessel, der in Metall oder Holz mit Lederpolsterung erhältlich ist. Die verschiedenen Materialien betonen die unterschiedlichen Aspekte des minimalistischen Rahmens die von einfacher Wärme zu strenger Geometrie reichen.

Metro² has long, fluid lines and versatile, modular elements, for a streamlined, modern approach to sofa design.

Die langgestreckten fließenden Linien und vielseitige modulare Elemente des Metro² ergeben ein stromlinienförmiges modernes Sofadesign.

Mex Cube's different elements can be combined to form different sofas. Backrest can be added or removed, and units can stand indivudally, alongside one another, or even facing each other.

Die unterschiedlichen Elemente von Mex Cube können zu verschiedenen Sofas zusammengesetzt werden. Rückenlehnen können hinzugefügt oder entfernt werden und die Elemente einzeln, nebeneinander oder auch gegenüber platziert werden.

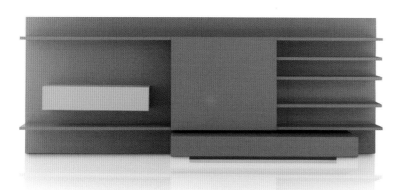

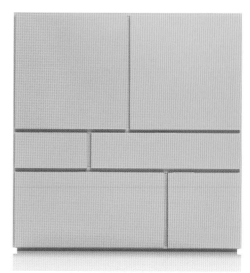

Modern is a storage system that includes a sideboard, a shelf, and a dresser. The main motif is the square, so that any arrangement of the different pieces remains geometrically harmonious.

Modern ist ein Aufbewahrungssystem zu dem ein Sideboard, ein Regal und eine Kommode gehören. Das Hauptmotiv ist ein Quadrat, so dass jede Zusammenstellung der Elemente geometrisch harmonisch erscheint.

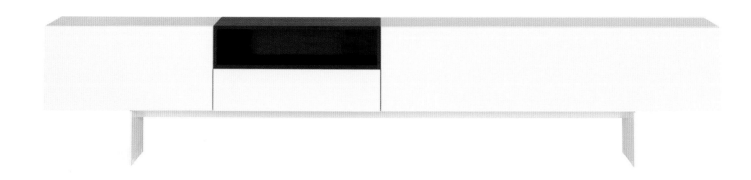

The T030 System relies on a set of panels and benches of different dimensions, set up on a base board, to create different storage solutions. Clear lines and structured asymmetry give it aesthetic flair.

Das T030 System besteht aus einer Reihe von Platten und Stufen in verschiedenen Größen, die auf einem Grundgestell aufliegen, wodurch sich verschiedene Aufbewahrungsmöglichkeiten ergeben. Klare Linien und eine strukturelle Asymmetrie machen seine Ästhetik aus.

The Dark Side of the Moon's laminated glass table-top comes in neutral tones, or in a dazzling mix of bright color strips, whose stained-glass effect transcends the simple structure.

Die Verbundglastischplatte des Dark Side of the Moon gibt es in neutralen Tönen oder mit brillanten Farbstreifen deren Buntglaseffekt über die einfache Struktur des Tisches hinausgeht.

The Frog Armchair and Lounge Chair have low-slung seats woven out of natural materials on a tubular steel frame, for an interesting mix of organic and industrial tones.

Sessel und Klubsessel Frog haben tiefe, aus natürlichen Materialien gewobene Sitze auf einem Stahlrohrrahmen, woraus ein interessanter Mix von organischen und industriellen Akzenten entsteht.

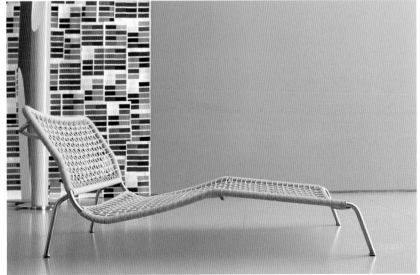

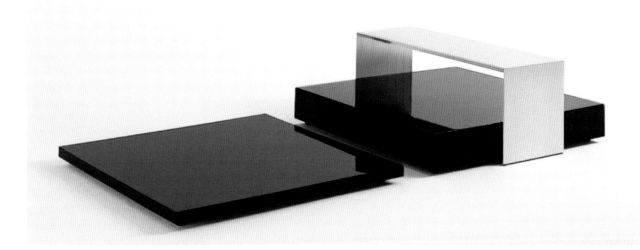

Note is a series of prismatic tables, which can be used individually or be superimposed to create table or storage landscapes within a room.

Note ist eine Reihe prismatischer Tische, die einzeln oder kombiniert zusammengestellt werden können um Tisch- und Aufbewahrungslandschaften in einem Raum zu erschaffen.

Radar allows its components to be exchanged, so that doors and drawers can alternate with open space. Playing with the volumes changes both Radar's appearance and function.

Die Komponenten von Radar können ausgetauscht werden, so dass sich Türen und Schubladen mit offenen Fächern abwechseln. Das Spiel mit den verschiedenen Volumen ändert jedes Mal das Aussehen und die Funktionalität des Systems.

Softwall takes the design and proportions of its predecessor, Wall, and rounds off the corners and angles for a softer look.

Softwall reflektiert das Design und die Proportionen seines Vorgängers Wall mit gerundeten Kanten und Ecken für eine weichere Optik.

Jelly's tubular, chromed-steel frame props a foam shell high up off the ground. The chair's padded backrests and armrests are the same height, creating a visually simple object.

Jelly's verchromter Stahlrohrrahmen hebt die Polyurethan-Kaltschaum Schale hoch über den Boden. Der gepolsterte Rücken und die Armlehnen sind auf der gleichen Höhe wodurch ein optisch klares Objekt entsteht.

The sleek .03 chair's back, seat, and front legs are all joined in one fluid line. The back legs provide support, and leaf springs in the foam shell provide comfort and flexibility.

Rücken, Sitz und Vorderbeine formen eine fließende Linie beim eleganten Stuhl .03. Die hinteren Beine geben Halt, während Bandfedern in der Schaumstoffschale für Gemütlichkeit und Flexibilität sorgen.

Maarten
van Severen

Maarten van Severen (June 5, 1956 – February 21, 2005) was a Belgian furniture designer. He studied architecture at the Sint-Lucas Art Academy in Ghent, Belgium, and soon began working for various interior design and furniture design companies in Belgium before creating his first furniture pieces in 1986. In 1987, he launched his own, independent studio in Ghent. His precise, hand-produced designs reflected his main motivation, which was the quest for perfection in form. Severen worked in a variety of different materials, including aluminum, Bakelite and polyester. The most famous of his designs is undoubtedly the ".03 chair", an understated icon of 20th century design. First mass-produced by Vitra in 1999, the ".03 chair" can now be found all over the world, equally at ease in the Centre Pom-

pidou in Paris and Sint-Baaf's Cathedral in Ghent as it is in McDonald's restaurants across Europe and the Seattle public library. Until the ".03 chair", mass-produced chairs were generally assembled from three separate components, namely the backrest, the seat, and the legs. Van Severen revolutionized the market with the creation of a chair which fuses the body of the chair and the front legs into a fluid line. 10 years in the making, the final Vitra model uses a foam material that adapts to the body, and leaf springs are integrated into the backrest to allow the sitter to lean back.

Maarten van Severen (5.6.1956–21.2.2005) war ein belgischer Möbeldesigner. Er studierte Architektur an der Sint-Lucas Art Academy in Gent, Belgien, und begann kurz darauf für verschiedene Innenarchitektur- und Möbeldesignfirmen in Belgien zu arbeiten. 1986 entwickelte er seine ersten Möbel und gründete 1987 sein eigenes unabhängiges Studio in Gent.

Seine präzisen, handgefertigten Entwürfe reflektieren seine innere Suche nach der perfekten Form. Severen arbeitete mit einer Vielzahl von Materialien, unter anderem mit Aluminium, Bakelit und Polyester. Seine berühmteste Arbeit ist der Stuhl „.03", ein schlichtes Design-Kultobjekt des 20. Jahrhunderts. Zum ersten Mal im Jahr 1999 serienmäßig von Vitra hergestellt, passt dieser Stuhl genauso gut in das Centre Pompidou in Paris und die Sint-Baaf's Kathedrale in Gent wie in McDonald's Restaurants in ganz Europa und die Bücherei von Seattle. Vor der Entwicklung des „.03 Stuhles", wurden serienmäßig produzierte Stühle aus drei einzelnen Komponenten zusammengesetzt, nämlich der Rückenlehne, dem Sitz und den Beinen. Van Severen revolutionierte den Markt, indem er einen Stuhl entwickelte, bei dem die Sitzfläche und die vorderen Beine zu einer fließenden Linie verbunden werden. Zehn Jahre nach der ersten Herstellung besteht das neueste Vitra-Modell aus einem Schaumstoff, der sich an den Körper anpasst, sowie Bandfedern, die in die Rückenlehnen eingearbeitet sind und so das Zurücklehnen ermöglichen.

.05 is van Severen's take on the cantilever chair. He combined his flexible foam shell with a the classic cantilevered, tubular steel frame.

Der .05 ist van Severens Version eines Freischwingers. Er kombiniert seine flexible Schaumstoffschale mit einem klassischen freischwingenden Stahlrohrrahmen.

The .04 chair places a flexible foam shell on a swivel base, but a special tilting mechanism also allows the sitter to rock back in the seat.

Beim Stuhl .04 ist eine flexible Schaumstoffschale auf einem Drehuntergestell positioniert, während ein spezieller Kippmechanismus es dem Nutzer auch erlaubt vor und zurück zu schaukeln.

The .06 chair takes the concept of the .05 to an even more comfortable level, lowering the seat and lengthening the cantilever base to create a gravity-defying lounge chair.

Der Stuhl .06 ist eine noch bequemere Variante des .05 mit niedrigerem Sitz und einem längeren Untergestell wodurch ein extrem freischwingender Sessel entsteht.

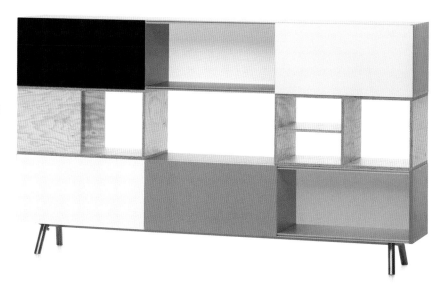

Kast combines shelves, cupboards with sliding doors, and two simple wooden crates to create a multi-functional storage system that alternates full and empty spaces for a highly geometric aesthetic.

Kast ist eine Kombination von Regalen, Schränken mit Schiebetüren sowie zwei einfachen Holzkisten wodurch ein vielfältiges Aufbewahrungssystem entsteht aus abwechselnd offenen und geschlossenen Elementen mit einer hoch geometrischen Ästhetik.

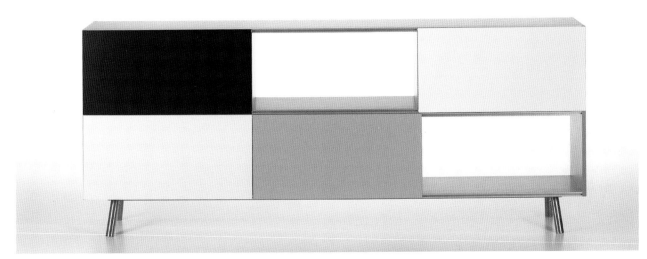

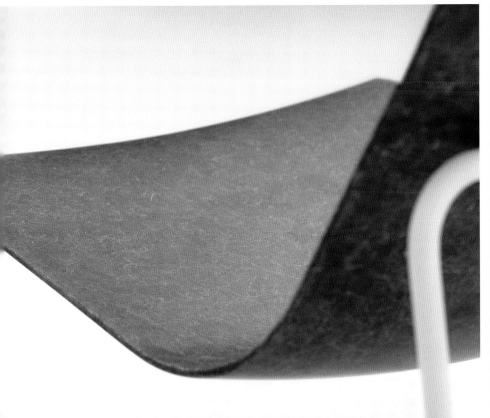

The LC03 lounge chair seems impossibly lightweight. A slim polyester seat is supported on slender metal legs, but the design follows the contour of the body and is both supportive and comfortable.

Der Sessel LC03 erscheint unglaublich leicht. Ein schmaler Polyestersitz wird von dünnen Metallbeinen getragen, mit einer Form die sich an die Konturen des Körpers anpasst und dabei gleichzeitig stützend und komfortabel ist.

The Open Chair, designed for outdoor use, is con-
structed entirely out of stainless steel. Perforated
steel sheets form the shell, which is supported by
a tubular steel frame.

Der Open Chair, für die Nutzung im Freien ent-
worfen, ist komplett aus Edelstahl gefertigt. Die
Schale ist aus gelochtem Stahlblech gefertigt und
wird von einem Stahlrohrrahmen gehalten.

James
Irvine

James Irvine (born in 1958 in London) is a British industrial designer working in Milan. After graduating from the Royal College of Art in 1984, Irvine moved to Milan to work as a design consultant for Olivetti, where he designed industrial products until 1992. In 1988, he opened his own design studio. Cappellini was one of his first clients, and since then he has gone on to work with B&B Italia, Magis, MDF, and Canon.

Showing a remarkable versatility, Irvine has designed everything from sofas to lamps, bus shelters, and even a garlic press. In 2000, he completed the design for the body of the new city bus for the city of Hanover, in collaboration with Mercedes-Benz, which produced 131 models of the bus. In 2004, he was elected Royal Designer for Industry by the Royal Society of Arts in London.

In addition to his independent design career, Irvine was also a professor of industrial design at the Hochschule für Gestaltung in Karlsruhe from 2005 to 2007.

James Irvine (geboren 1958 in London) ist ein britischer Industriedesigner, der in Mailand tätig ist.

Nach seinem Studium am Royal College of Art zog Irvine 1984 nach Mailand um als Entwurfsberater für Olivetti zu arbeiten. Dort entwarf er industrielle Produkte bis zum Jahr 1992. 1988 eröffnete er außerdem sein eigenes Designstudio. Cappellini war einer seiner ersten Kunden und seit diesem Zeitpunkt arbeitet er außerdem mit B&B Italia, Magis, MDF, und Canon zusammen.

Mit einer erstaunlichen Vielseitigkeit entwirft Irvine alle möglichen Dinge, von Sofas bis hin zu Leuchten, Bushaltestellen und sogar eine Knoblauchpresse. Im Jahr 2000 entwickelte er in Zusammenarbeit mit der Firma Mercedes-Benz die Karosserie eines neuen Stadtbusses für die Stadt Hannover, wovon 131 Modelle produziert wurden.

2004 wurde er von der Royal Society of Arts (Königliche Gesellschaft zur Förderung der Künste) in London zum Royal Designer for Industry (Königlichen Industriedesigner) gewählt.

Neben seiner Karriere als Designer war Irvine von 2005 bis 2007 auch als Professor für Industrielles Design an der Hochschule für Gestaltung in Karlsruhe tätig.

The Open Series, which also includes a table, skill-fully shapes steel into soft, graceful shapes.

Für die Open Series Kollektion, zu der auch ein Tisch gehört, wurde Stahl kunstfertig zu weichen, graziösen Formen verarbeitet.

S 123 is an elegant and practical bar stool, whose main element is tubular steel. The steel loop serves as a footrest, and the round base is complemented by the round or oval seat.

S 123 ist ein eleganter, praktischer Barhocker, der hauptsächlich aus Stahlrohr besteht. Die Stahlschlinge dient als Fußstütze, während das runde Untergestell durch einen runden oder ovalen Sitz vervollständigt wird.

S 5002 converts a the classic daybed shape into both a sofa and a chaise longue thanks to the addition of simple, upholstered elements that form armrests and backrests.

Die klassische Schlafcouch-Form des S 5002 kann in ein Sofa oder eine Chaiselongue verwandelt werden, indem einfache gepolsterte Elemente hinzugefügt werden, die den Rücken und die Armlehnen bilden.

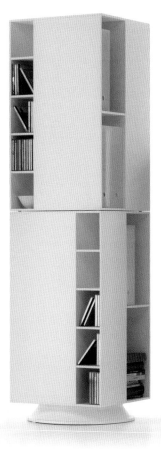

Box is a set of multifunctional, stackable storage units, which stand on swivel bases. The different wooden units are optimized for different functions.

Box ist ein Set von vielseitigen, stapelbaren Aufbewahrungseinheiten auf drehbaren Unterge- stellen. Die verschiedenen Holzelemente sind für unterschiedliche Funktionen optimiert.

The Egal shelf features compartments of four different heights, which can be stacked freely within the frame. Sliding doors can be added to the individual compartments.

Das Regal Egal hat Fächer in vier verschiedenen Höhen, die frei im Rahmen platziert werden können. Schiebetüren können zusätzlich an den einzelnen Fächern angebracht werden.

Axel
Kufus

Axel Kufus (born in 1958 in Essen) is a German designer currently working in Berlin. After completing his studies in carpentry and design, along with some collaborations in bronze work, he began creating his own furniture at the CrelleWerkstatt in Berlin. He soon gained a reputation as a leading force in New German Design, which was a movement challenging the functionalism that ruled the design world in the 1980s. In Germany in particular, the focus was shifted away from "good form" and towards an aesthetic that owed more to collage and a sense of fracture. Kufus first gained icon status in 1989 with the "FNP" shelving system. The modular, minimalist shelving system, which can be expanded and modified to fit different environments and requirements, is still produced today by Nils Holger Moormann.

Since 1993, Kufus has also had a successful career in teaching, first as a professor of product design at the Bauhaus University of Weimar, and then teaching at the Berlin University of the Arts.

Axel Kufus (geboren 1958 in Essen) ist ein deutscher Designer, der in Berlin tätig ist. Nach einer Bau- und Möbelschreinerlehre, einem Design-Studium an der Hochschule der Künste in Berlin sowie der Zusammenarbeit mit kreativen Bronzewerkstätten begann er eigene Möbel in der CrelleWerkstatt Berlin zu entwerfen und produzieren.

Er wurde bald als eine treibende Kraft des Neuen Deutschen Designs angesehen, einer Bewegung, die den vorherrschenden Funktionalismus der 1980er Jahre in Frage stellte. Vor allem in Deutschland wurde der Schwerpunkt weniger auf „Gute Form" gelegt als auf eine Ästhetik, die mehr auf Kollagen und künstlerischen Brüchen basierte. Kufus errang 1989 zum ersten Mal Kultstatus mit seinem „FNP"-Regalsystem. Dieses modulare minimalistische Regalsystem, das erweitert und an verschiedene Umgebungen und Bedürfnisse angepasst werden kann, wird heute noch von Nils Holger Moormann produziert.

Seit 1993 machte Kufus auch erfolgreich Karriere als Hochschuldozent, zunächst als Professor für Produktdesign an der Fakultät Gestaltung, Bauhaus Universität Weimar, und danach als Professor für „Entwerfen und Entwickeln im Design" an der Universität der Künste Berlin.

Egal's compartments can be assembled in different directions, so that the shelving system can take on an endless variety of dimensions.

Die Fächer des Egal-Systems können in verschiedenen Richtungen kombiniert werden, wodurch das Regal eine endlose Vielfalt an Dimensionen bekommt.

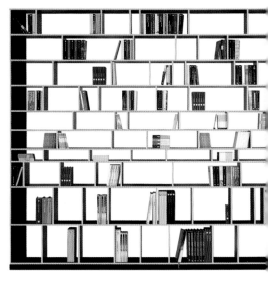

Lader is a modular storage system in which drawers are combined with four different sizes of frames to create individualized storage solutions. Lader can also be mounted on a wall.

Lader ist ein modulares Aufbewahrungssystem mit Schubladen, die mit vier verschiedenen Größen oder Rahmen kombiniert werden können, um individuelle Aufbewahrungslösungen zu schaffen. Lader kann auch an der Wand angebracht werden.

The FNP shelf is made up only of wooden panels, for a structure so minimalist that it becomes transparent, almost disappearing when the shelves are filled.

Das Regal FNP besteht nur aus Wangen und Böden mit einer solch minimalistischen Struktur, die transparent wirkt und fast verschwindet, wenn das Regale benutzt wird.

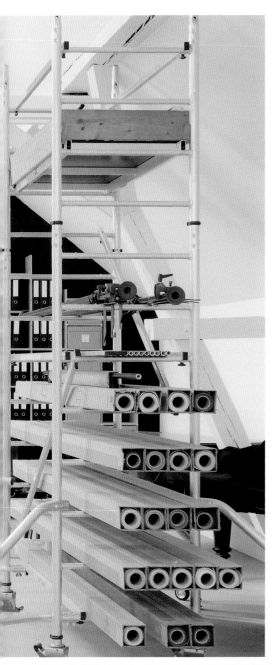

The Basel Chair is an innovative take on the classic wooden chair. Adding a molded plastic backrest and seat to the wooden frame results in an engaging combination of organic and synthetic materials.

Der Stuhl Basel ist eine innovative Variante des klassischen Holstuhls. Das Hinzufügen von einem geformten Kunststoffrücken und Sitz zu dem hölzernen Rahmen ergibt eine überzeugende Kombination von organischen und synthetischen Materialien.

Jasper
Morrison

Jasper Morrison (born in 1959, in London) is a British product and furniture designer. After completing his studies in design at Kingston Polytechnic Design School and The Royal College of Art, Morrison set up an office in London in 1986. He soon began designing a wide range of products for different companies, including the German door handle producers FSB, and the furniture companies Vitra and Cappellini. In 1992, Morrison and his friend James Irvine created the "Progetto Ogetto" for Cappellini, which was a collection of household objects designed by a group of young European designers. In 1995, Morrison was commissioned to design the new Hanover Tram, for which he received the IF Transportation Design Prize and the Ecology award at the Hanover Industrial Fair.

Morrison's elegant and quietly witty style has gained him much recognition over the course of his career. His diverse range of products and clients has allowed him to experiment with new materials and techniques. The "Low Pad Chair", for example, designed for Cappellini, was inspired by Poul Kjaerholm's classic steel and leather chair, but Morrison used new upholstery methods to create a padded leather seat that is both comfortable and durable. His most recent projects include new furniture for Tate Modern in London, as well as exhibits in Paris and Tokyo.

Jasper Morrison (geboren 1959 in London) ist ein britischer Produkt- und Möbeldesigner. Nach seinem Studium an der Kingston Polytechnic Design School und dem Royal College of Art gründete Morrison im Jahre 1986 ein Designstudio in London. Er entwickelte eine Reihe von Produkten für verschiedene Firmen wie dem deutschen Türbeschlaghersteller FSB und den Möbelmarken Vitra und Cappellini. 1992 entwickelten Morrison und sein Freund James Irvine die „Progetto Ogetto" Serie für Cappellini, eine Kollektion von Haushaltsartikeln, die von einer Gruppe von jungen europäischen Designern entworfen wurde. 1995 wurde Morrison beauftragt, die neue Stadtbahn von Hannover zu entwickeln, für welche er den IF Transportation Design Preis und den Ecology Design Award auf der Hannover Messe erhielt.

Morrisons eleganter und leicht ironischer Stil wurde im Laufe seiner Karriere sehr gewürdigt. Seine Vielfalt an Produkten, aber auch an Kunden, ermöglichte es ihm, mit immer neuen Materialien und Methoden zu experimentieren. Sein „Low Pad Chair" zum Beispiel, den er für Cappellini entwarf, war von Poul Kjærholms klassischem Stahl- und Ledersessel inspiriert, wobei Morrison neuartige Polstermethoden benutzte, um einen gepolsterten Ledersitz herzustellen, der gleichzeitig bequem und langlebig ist. Zu seinen jüngsten Projekten gehören neue Möbel für das Tate Modern in London sowie für Ausstellungen in Paris und Tokio.

The HAL chair comes in many versions, with wooden or metal legs, a four-legged frame or a cantilevered frame, and with or without a fabric cover. The versatile shape, however, remains the same.

Den Stuhl HAL gibt es vielen Varianten: mit hölzernen oder Metallbeinen, einem vierbeinigen oder freischwingenden Rahmen, sowie mit oder ohne Stoffbezug. Die vielseitige Form bleibt allerdings immer gleich.

The Trattoria Chair pairs a rustic, solid beech frame with a brightly-colored, slightly translucent polycarbonate seat and backrest.

Der Stuhl Trattoria verbindet einen rustikalen, massiven Buchenholzrahmen mit farbenfrohen, transluzenten Sitz und Rückenlehne aus Polykarbonat.

The Pad Family includes Hi Pad and Low Pad,
who share polyurethane foam shells and two steel
frames that form the legs. Low Pad is a lounge
chair with a headrest, while High Pad is an office
chair.

Zur Pad Reihe gehören Hi Pad und Low Pad,
welche beide aus PU-Schaum-Schalen und zwei
Stahlrahmen als Beine bestehen. Low Pad ist ein
Klubsessel mit einer Kopfstütze, während Hi Pad
ein Bürostuhl ist.

The Lotus Family is series of office swivel chairs, which comes with or without armrests, and with high or low backs. The ergonomic, ridged upholstery unites the different versions.

Die Lotus Serie besteht aus Bürostühlen welche mit ohne Armlehnen und mit hohen oder niedrigen Rücken erhältlich sind. Die ergonomisch geformte steife Polsterung vereint die verschiedenen Versionen.

The Folding Air-Chair is made of three components: the front legs and the backrest are one single piece, onto which the seat is hinged, and another frame adds support in the back.

Der zusammenfaltbare Air-Chair besteht aus drei Teilen: die Vorderbeine und Rückenlehne sind ein einziges Stück an welchem der Sitz eingehängt ist, während ein weiterer Rahmen den Rücken stützt.

The three members of the Cork Family can serve as stools or side tables. The lightweight material makes the remarkably easy to handle, without sacrificing durability.

Die drei Teile der Cork Serie können als Hocker oder Beistelltische verwendet werden. Das leichte Material macht sie sehr leicht zu handhaben ohne dass auf Langlebigkeit verzichtet wird.

The Superoblong Sofa is a system of large, freestanding elements that are connected to each other using zippers. The modules are actually filled with polystyrene beans, so that they look and feel like large pillows.

Das Sofa Superoblong ist ein System aus großen, freistehenden Elementen, die mit Reißverschlüssen verbunden werden. Die einzelnen Bausteine sind mit Styroporperlen gefüllt so dass sie sich wie große Kissen anfühlen und aussehen.

The rectangular Elan sofa hovers above the ground on slender, tubular steel legs. A wooden frame supports polyurethane foam upholstering and feather cushions.

Das rechteckige Sofa Elan schwebt auf schlanken Stahlrohrbeinen über dem Boden. Ein hölzerner Rahmen unterstützt die PU-Schaum Polster und Federkissen.

The lightweight Sim Chair has a flexible chromed-steel frame. The legs and the back of the chair are one continuous piece, with two smaller bars added for support. The seat and backrest are plastic.

Der leichte Stuhl Sim hat einen flexiblen verchromten Stahlrahmen. Die Beine und Rücken des Stuhls bestehen aus einem einzelnen durchgängigen Stück, mit zwei kleinen Stangen als zusätzliche Stützen. Sitz und Rückenlehne sind aus Kunststoff.

Monopod exudes a sense of stability. The chair is anchored to the floor by a heavy base, and the seat and backrest fold slightly inwards, almost protectively.

Monopod vermittelt das Gefühl von Stabilität. Der Sessel ist mit einem schweren Sockel am Boden verankert, Sitz und Rückenlehne formen eine schützende Sphäre.

The Atlas System is a set of lightweight metal tables, with aluminum and laminate tops, and aluminum bases.

Das System Atlas besteht aus leichten Metalltischen mit Aluminium- oder HPL-beschichteten Platten und Aluminium-Untergestellen.

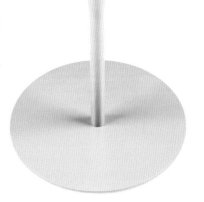

The Crate Armchair was inspired by wine crates,
whose character can be seen in the wooden
slats that form the shell of the chair. These are
balanced in a gentle curve within a painted metal
frame.

Der Sessel Crate Armchair wurde von Weinkisten
inspiriert die den Holzleisten ähneln die die Schale
des Stuhles bilden. Diese sind zu einer sanften
Wölbung gebogen innerhalb eines lackierten
Metallrahmens gebogen.

The unusual the Fjord Armchair reveals its practicality slowly, through use. The backrest and arms fit to the sitter's body, and the lightweight foam frame swivels effortlessly.

Der außergewöhnliche Sessel Fjord zeigt seine praktischen Seiten nach und nach. Die Rückenlehne und Arme passen sich dem Körper des Nutzers an während der leichte Schaumstoffrahmen sich mühelos drehen lässt.

Patricia
Urquiola

Patricia Urquiola (born in 1961 in Oviedo) is a Spanish-born architect and designer currently working in Milan. She graduated from the Technical University of Madrid in 1989, then went on to become Achille Castiglioni's assistant lecturer at the Polytechnic Institute of Milan and at the E.N.S.C.I in Paris. In 1990, she embarked on her own career in product development at DePadova, and as an associate in an architecture firm. In 1996, she became head of the Lissoni Associati Design group, and she has since successfully launched several of her own furniture designs with B&B Italia, Moroso, and Molteni. A selection of her products were featured at the Italian Design Exhibition in 2001. Her elegant, upholstered pieces have met with worldwide acclaim, and she is considered to be a leading figure in Italian design, despite her Spanish background. Many of her designs, especially sofas like the "Bend" sofa and the "Highlands" sofa, feature exchangeable elements, which can be set up according to individual preferences. The piece then becomes a tool for creating a specific environment, instead of a static object.

Patricia Urquiola (geboren 1961 in Oviedo) ist eine spanische Architektin und Designerin, die in Mailand tätig ist.

Sie promovierte 1989 am Polytechnikum in Mailand und arbeitete danach als wissenschaftliche Assistentin von Achille Castiglioni am Polytechnikum von Mailand und dem E.N.S.C.I in Paris. 1990 startete sie ihre Karriere in der Produktentwicklung bei DePadova und als Teilhaberin eines Architekturbüros. 1996 wurde sie Leiterin der Designergruppe Lissoni Associati. Außerdem hat sie zwischenzeitlich erfolgreich eigene Möbelentwürfe in Zusammenarbeit mit B&B Italia, Moroso und Molteni herausgebracht. Eine Auswahl ihrer Produkte wurde auf der italienischen Design-Messe 2001 gezeigt. Ihre eleganten Polstermöbel sind weltweit beliebt. Trotz ihres spanischen Hintergrundes wird sie allgemein als eine der führenden Persönlichkeiten des italienischen Designs angesehen. Viele ihrer Möbel, besonders Sofas wie „Bend" und „Highlands", haben austauschbare Elemente, die nach den persönlichen Vorlieben eingestellt werden können. Das Möbelstück ist somit kein statischer Gegenstand, sondern ein Instrument zum Gestalten einer persönlichen Umgebung.

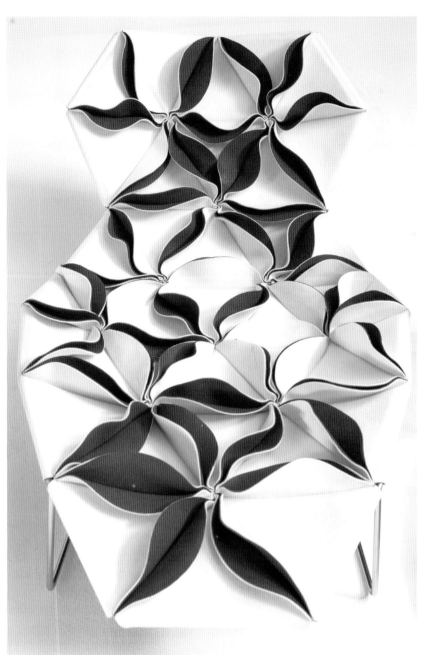

The Antibodi Lounge Chair features triangular pieces of fabric that are sewn together in a cellular pattern. These elements can face outwards for a 3D effect, or inwards for a more subdued aesthetic.

Die Liege Antibodi besteht aus Stoffdreiecken, die in einer Zellenstruktur zusammengenäht sind. Diese Elemente können nach außen zeigen für eine 3D-Effekt oder nach innen, für eine etwas mildere Ästhetik.

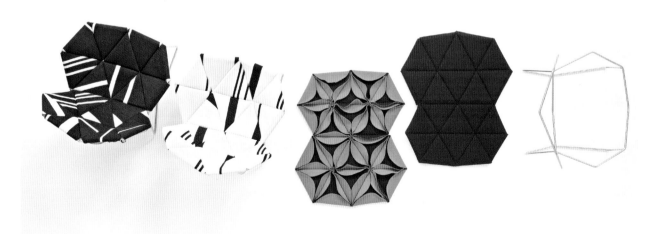

Bend Sofa's massive forms seem to have been sculpted rather than assembled. The modular seating elements can be arranged in different ways, and the curved volumes give any arrangement an organic feel.

Die massive Form des Sofas Bend scheint eher gemeißelt als zusammengefügt zu sein. Die modularen Sitzelemente können auf verschiedene Arten kombiniert werden, während die gebogenen Formen einen organischen Eindruck vermitteln.

The Lowland Sofa is an experiment in deconstruction. The seats, backrests, and armrests are all independent pieces that stand alone on stainless steel feet.

Das Sofa Lowland ist ein Experiment der Dekonstruktion. Die Sitze, Rückenlehnen und Armlehnen sind alles einzelne Teile die frei auf Aluminiumbeinen stehen.

Lowseat is a set of single seating modules that can stand alone, or be grouped into larger arrangements. Each piece stands on stainless steel legs.

Lowseat ist eine Reihe einzelner Sitzmodule die frei platziert oder in größeren Ensembles zusammengesetzt werden können. Jedes Stück steht auf Edelstahlbeinen.

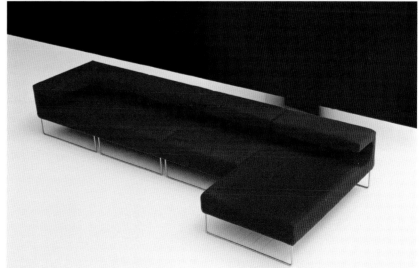

The Silver Lake's solid, polygonal volumes are more reminiscent of mid-century design than Urquiola's other creations. The wood frames of the sofas and armchairs contrast nicely with the fabric seats.

Die massiven mehreckigen Volumen von Silver Lake erinnern an das Design der 1950er Jahre. Die Holzrahmen der Sofas und Sessel kontrastieren mit den Stoffsitzen.

The Bloomy Armchair got its name because its organic form looks like the beginning of a flower, sprouting up from the ground and extending its petals. The foam chair comes with a removable cover.

Der Sessel Bloomy wurde nach seiner organischen Form benannt, die einer Bllüte ähnelt die gerade aus dem Boden hervorwächst und ihre Blütenblätter ausstreckt. Der Schaumstoffsessel hat einen abnehmbaren Bezug.

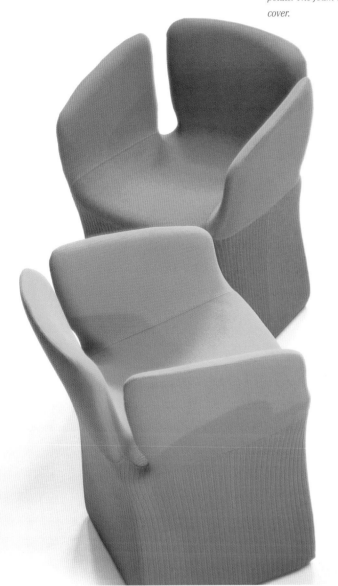

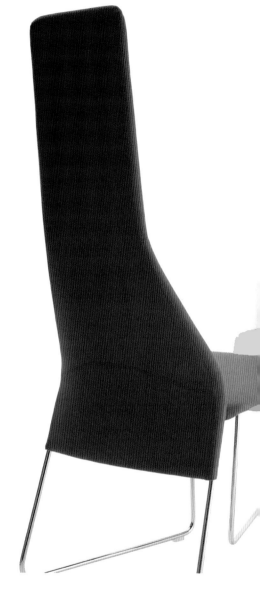

The Lazy collection includes a bed and a range of chairs. The single or double bed, Lazy-Night, features and extra high headboard, with an adjustable elastic strap on which cushions can be attached.

Zu der Lazy Kollektion gehört ein Bett und eine Reihe von Stühlen. Das Einzel- und Doppelbett Lazy-Night hat ein extra hohes Kopfende mit einem einstellbaren elastischen Gurt an welchem Kissen befestigt werden können.

The Lazy seating collection includes an easy chair, a high-back chair, stools, and an armchair. The chairs' funky curves and angles are upholstered in soft fabric, perfect for lazy lounging.

Zur Sitzmöbelkollektion Lazy gehören ein Polstersessel, ein Sessel mit hohem Rücken, Hocker und ein Armlehnsessel. Die unkonventionellen Wölbungen und Winkel sind mit weichem Stoff bezogen der perfekt für entspanntes Liegen geeignet ist.

The Shanghai Tip Sofa's simple lines are complemented by the muted color range, with bright
accents from the cushions. Raised off the floor
with steel legs, the sofa also has an adjustable
backrest.

Die schlichten Linien des Sofas Shanghai Tip sind
ergänzt von einer Auswahl an gedämpften Farben,
mit Kissen als leuchtende Akzente. Mithilfe von
Stahlbeinen über dem Boden schwebend, hat das
Sofa auch eine verstellbare Rückenlehne.

The evocative Smock Armchair, with intricate
folds in the fabric draped over the ring-shaped
armrests, feels almost like a hammock. The
cover can be removed entirely, and also comes in
leather.

Der innovative Sessel Smock mit seinen aufwändi-
gen Stofffalten über den ringförmigen Armlehnen
fühlt sich fast wie eine Hängematte an. Der Bezug
kann ganz abgenommen werden und es gibt ihn
auch in Leder.

The Fat Fat series includes a sofa, a high-backed easy chair, and versatile forms that are ottomans, stools, or even tables. The soft, round shapes remain solid, supportive, and endlessly inviting.

Zu der Fat Fat Serie gehört ein Sofa, ein Polstersessel mit hohem Rücken und verschiedene Elemente die als Ottomane, Hocker oder sogar Tische dienen. Die weichen runden Formen sind immer fest, stützend und unendlich einladend.

The Canasta outdoor furniture range includes several sofas and chairs, as well as tables. The seating elements are tied together through their summery, basket-like frames.

Zu der Außenmöbel Kollektion Canasta gehören verschiedene Sofas und Stühle, sowie Tische. Die Sitzelemente sind durch ihre sommerlichen korbähnlichen Rahmen zusammengehalten.

The Canasta table is more geometric, but the visually light design, tiled tabletop and painted patterns also give it a warm-weather feel.

Der Tisch Canasta ist geometrisch geformt, aber seine optisch leichte, geflieste Tischplatte mit gemaltem Muster verleihen ihm ein Schönwetter-Gefühl.

Tufty-Too is a sofa system of block-shaped seating
islands with removable fabric covers. The set
includes a chaise longue, ottoman, and corner
sofa pieces, all with the distinctive plush detailing.

Tufty-Too ist ein Sofa System aus blockartigen
Sitzinseln mit abziehbaren Stoffbezügen. Zu dem
Set gehört eine Chaiselongue, Ottomane und
Ecksofaelemente die alle unverkennbare Plüschde-
tails aufweisen.

Spring is a sofa of stark geometry and massive
volumes. The seats, backrests and armrests are
simply different dimensions of the same basic
shape, creating a harmonious uniformity.

Spring ist ein stark geometrisches Sofa mit
massiven Formen. Die Sitze, Rückenlehne und
Armlehnen sind einfach verschiedene Dimensionen derselben Grundform, was eine harmonische
Einheit ergibt.

Springfield is Spring's predecessor, with slightly leaner volumes. The different elements are connected with metal joints, and the small gaps between pieces highlight their precise forms.

Springfield ist der Vorläufer des Spring mit etwas schmaleren Dimensionen. Die verschiedenen Elemente sind durch Metallscharniere verbunden. Kleine Fugen zwischen den Elementen unterstreichen ihre präzisen Formen.

Blossom ceiling lights are a series of hanging lamps with small variations in size, shapes and colors, which can easily be hung in groups, like a bouquet of flowers.

Blossom Deckenleuchten sind eine Reihe von Hängelampen mit unterschiedlichen Größen, Formen und Farben, die man leicht in Gruppen wie einen Blumenstrauß aufhängen kann.

Hella
Jongerius

Hella Jongerius (born in 1963 in de Meern) is a Dutch designer. After studying at the Academy for Industrial Deisgn in Eindhoven, she created her own design studio, Jongeriuslab, in 1993. Today, her main claim to fame is her deft fusion of industry and craftwork, which results in designs that incorporate traditional aesthetics with contemporary flair. "Bovist", the multi-purpose object which can serve as a floor cushion, a stool or an ottoman features large-scale embroidery, inspired by many different references. The "Lacemaker" version, for example, is a take on "The Laceworker" by Johannes Vermeer. The original craftwork is seamlessly integrated into an industrially sound piece of furniture.

Her work has been shown in museums and galleries around the world, notably the Museum of Modern Art in New York and the Galerie Kreo in Paris. In addition to her independent projects, she has produced furniture and design pieces for clients such as Belux and Vitra as well as Ikea.

Hella Jongerius (geb. 1963 in de Meern) ist eine niederländische Designerin. Nach ihrem Studium an der Academy for Industrial Design in Eindhoven gründete sie im Jahr 1993 ihr eigenes Designstudio, das „Jongeriuslab".

Das herausragende Merkmal ihrer Arbeit ist das geschickte Verschmelzen von Industrie und Handwerk, wodurch Designs entstehen, die traditionelle Ästhetik mit zeitgenössischem Flair vereinen. „Bovist", ein Mehrzweckobjekt, das als Bodenkissen, Hocker oder Ottomane fungieren kann, ist mit großflächiger Stickerei verziert, die von vielen verschiedenen Referenzen inspiriert ist. So bezieht sich die „Spitzenklöpplerin"-Version z.B. auf das Gemälde „Die Spitzenklöpplerin" von Johannes Vermeer. Die originale Handarbeit ist dabei nahtlos in ein industriell produziertes Möbelstück integriert.

Zusätzlich zu ihren selbständigen Projekten entwirft sie auch Möbel und Designobjekte für Kunden wie Belux, Vitra und Ikea.

Ihre Arbeiten werden in Museen und Galerien rund um die Welt gezeigt, insbesondere auch im Museum of Modern Art in New York und der Galerie Kreo in Paris.

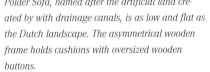

Polder Sofa, named after the artificial land created by with drainage canals, is as low and flat as the Dutch landscape. The asymmetrical wooden frame holds cushions with oversized wooden buttons.

Das Sofa Polder, das nach den künstlichen Landflächen, die durch Entwässerungskanäle entstehen, benannt ist, ist genauso niedrig und flach wie die holländische Landschaft. Der asymmetrische Holzrahmen enthält Kissen mit überdimensionalen Knöpfen.

Bovist is an embroidered pouf or ottoman, which sits firmly on the floor. The body is filled with small plastic balls, covered with different fabrics, and embroidered with the help of a computer.

Bovist ist ein besticktes Bodensitzkissen oder Hocker, der fest auf dem Boden aufliegt. Seine Füllung besteht aus kleinen Kunststoffkugeln, während seine Hülle aus verschiedenfarbigen Stoffen genäht und mit Computer-Stickereien verziert ist.

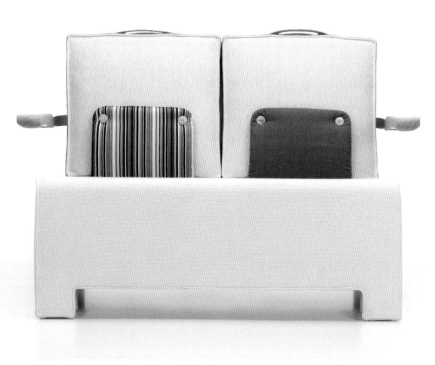

The Worker Sofa seems to sit especially low to
the ground, with most of its weight in the block-
shaped base. The frame is left visible, for a rustic
feel.

Das Sofa Worker scheint besonders niedrig zu
sein, wobei sich der größte Teil seines Gewichts
in dem quaderförmigen Untergestell befindet. Der
sichtbare Rahmen bewirkt einen rustikalen Effekt.

The Cube system consists of different chests of
drawers which can be configured into one unit
according to personal preference.

*Das System Cube besteht aus verschiedenen
Kommoden, die je nach den persönlichen Vorlieben des Benutzers zu modularen Aufbewahrungs-
systemen zusammengesetzt werden können.*

Werner
Aisslinger

Werner Aisslinger (born in 1964 in Berlin) is a German furniture designer. He graduated from the Berlin University of Arts in 1991, with a degree in design, and went on to work as a freelance designer for Ron Arad and Jasper Morrison in London. In 1993, he founded Studio Aisslinger, and soon established partnerships with Cappellini, Vitra, Interlübke, and Porro, among others. He works primarily in synthetic materials like fibreglass, gels, aluminium foam, neoprene, with the belief that good design must also be a quest for new materi-als and new technologies. In fact, he has introduced new materials to the design world himself: the "Juli" chair, for example, was ground-breaking in its use of polyurethane integral foam, which had never been used in furniture before. The "Juli" chair became the first chair by a German designer to be included as a permanent exhibit at the Museum of Modern Art in New York since 1964. He has won a number of awards during his career, including the Compasso d'Oro and the Design Prize of the Federal Republic of Germany.

Werner Aisslinger (geb. 1964 in Berlin) ist ein deutscher Möbeldesigner. 1991 schloss er sein Design-Studium an der Hochschule der Künste in Berlin ab und arbeitete danach freiberuflich für Ron Arad und Jasper Morrison in London. 1993 gründete er sein Studio Aisslinger und baute bald Partnerschaften mit Cappellini, Vitra, Interlübke, Porro, u.a. auf. Er arbeitet hauptsächlich mit synthetischen Materialien wie Fiberglas, Gels, Aluminium, Schaum und Neopren, basierend auf seiner Überzeugung, dass gutes Design auch eine Suche nach neuen Technologien und Materialien beinhalten muss. Tatsächlich hat er auch neue Materialien für die Designwelt entwickelt: So ist zum Beispiel der Stuhl „Juli" ein Vorreiter in der Verwendung von Polyurethan Integralschaum, der noch nie zuvor für Möbel verwendet worden war. Deshalb war dieser Stuhl seit 1964 der erste Stuhl eines deutschen Designers, der in die ständige Sammlung des Museum of Modern Art in New York aufgenommen wurde.

Aisslinger gewann eine Reihe von Preisen und Auszeichnungen, unter anderem den Compasso d'Oro sowie den Designpreis der Bundesrepublik Deutschland.

Different drawers can be opened in different directions, so the Cube can be placed anyhwere in the room.

Einzelne Schubladen können in verschiedene Richtungen geöffnet werden, wodurch die Cube Elemente überall im Zimmer aufgestellt werden können.

As its name implies, the Endless can be expanded indefinitely. New panels can be added to the joint system in any direction, allowing each owner to build into infinity.

Der Name ist Programm: Endless kann unendlich erweitert werden. Neue Paneele können in jeder Richtung an das Regalsystem angefügt werden, sodass jeder Besitzer sein eigenes „unendliches" Regal erstellen kann.

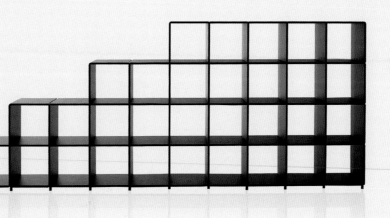

The Juli armchair's polyurethane body is perched on a chromed metal base. It can now also be upholstered in leather.

Die ausgeformte PU-Schale des Sessels Juli schwebt über einem verchromten Metallfuß. Es gibt ihn auch in einer lederbezogenen Version.

The basic building block for Level 34 is a 34-cm high bench. Containers, bins, and shelving systems fit on top of the bench, several benches can be used together, and soon an entire office landscape is ready to use.

Der Grundbaustein von Level 34 ist eine 34 cm hohe Bank, auf die Behälter, Ablagen, und Regalsysteme passen. Mehrere Bänke können zusammengefügt werden, so dass eine ganze Bürolandschaft entsteht.

Plus Unit is made up of individual drawers which can be stacked on top of each other attached side by side. Its modular nature makes it a versatile piece that can fit any room and any use.

Plus Unit besteht aus einzelnen Schubladen, die aufeinander gestapelt oder seitlich verbunden werden können. Sein Baukastenprinzip macht es zu einem vielseitigen Möbelstück, das in jeden Raum und zu jeder Art von Verwendung passt.

The X-Table seems simultaneously lightweight and massive. A heavy wooden slab rests on top of two x-shaped bases, but the final piece looks spontaneous and casual.

Der X-Table erscheint massiv, aber gleichzeitig leicht. Eine schwere Holzplatte ruht auf zwei X-förmigen Füßen und dennoch erscheint das Endprodukt spontan und lässig.

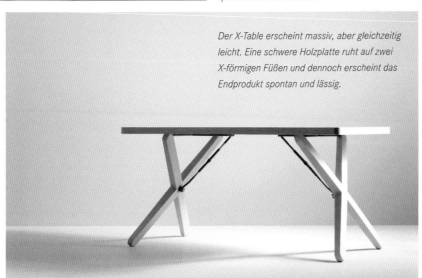

The shell-like seating element's material was determined after it was completely designed on the computer; fiberglass and resin created the visual transparency of the Osorom.

Das schalenähnliche Material des Sitzmöbels wurde ausgewählt, nachdem der Entwurf am Computer fertiggestellt war. Die Kombination von Glasfaser und Harz ergibt die optische Transparenz von Osorom.

Konstantin
Grcic

Konstantin Grcic (born in 1965 in Munich) is a German industrial designer. After training as a cabinet maker at Parnham College in England, he went on to the Royal College of Art in London, where he studied design. In 1991, he set up his own practice, Konstantin Grcic Industrial Design (KGID) in his native Munich. Since then, he has developed furniture, household products and lighting for some of Europe's leading design companies, including, ClassiCon, Magis, and Moroso. His pared down, minimalist style has met with great success, in part because he succeeds in bringing human sensibilty and humor to his take on formal strictness, so that even the most functional products display individual charm and a personal touch. The stackable "Monza" chair is formed by an engaging connection of Pop aesthetic and classic wood construction techniques. The injection-moulded plastic backrest is available in a variety of bright colors, which stand out against the subdued ash frame. Over the years, Grcic has received a number of coveted awards, including the Compasso d'Oro in 2001 and in 2011, for the "Myto" moulded plastic chair.

Konstantin Grcic (geb. 1965 in München) ist ein deutscher Industriedesigner. Im Anschluss an seine Ausbildung zum Möbelschreiner am Parnham College in England studierte er Design am Royal College of Art in London. 1991 gründete er sein eigenes Designbüro „Konstantin Grcic Industrial Design" (KGID) in seiner Heimatstadt München. In der Folge entwarf er Möbel, Leuchten und Accessoires im Auftrag zahlreicher führender Möbelmarken wie ClassiCon, Magis und Moroso.

Sein schlichter, minimalistischer Stil ist sehr erfolgreich, teilweise auch deshalb, weil es ihm gelingt, menschliche Empfindsamkeit und Humor mit seiner Art von formeller Strenge zu kombinieren, so dass sogar die funktionellsten Produkte einen individuellen Charme und eine persönliche Note bekommen. Der stapelbare Stuhl „Monza" bietet eine bestechende Kombination aus Pop-Ästhetik und klassischer Holzbearbeitungsmethoden. Die Rückenlehnen aus Kunststoff-Spritzguss gibt es in vielen leuchtenden Farben, die mit dem matten Eschenholzrahmen kontrastieren.

Im Laufe der Zeit erhielt Grcic viele begehrte Auszeichnungen, unter anderem den Compasso d'Oro im Jahr 2001 und im Jahr 2011 für den Spritzguss-Kunststoffstuhl „Myto".

The geometry of the Mars chair is made up of unusual slopes and edges. It has a slight inclination on the backseat and a low, hollow seat completely covered in fabric or leather.

Die Geometrie des Stuhles Mars besteht aus ungewöhnlichen Neigungen und Kanten. Der hintere Teil ist leicht abschüssig mit einem niedrigen hohlen Sitz, der komplett mit Stoff oder Leder bezogen ist.

Orcus is a foldout secretary desk with a black leather writing-pad, fodrawers, six shelves and a secret compartment.

Orcus ist ein ausklappbarer Sekretär mit einer Schreibplatte, vier Schubladen, sechs Regalen und einem Geheimfach.

The Venus chair is a combination of two bright wooden shells counterbalancing each other, with smooth and clear contours. It is designed for conference or dining rooms.

Der Stuhl Venus ist eine Kombination aus zwei Holzschalen, die sich gegenseitig mit glatten, klaren Konturen ausgleichen. Er wurde für Konferenzräume oder Esszimmer entworfen.

The Monza armchair is a combination of wood and plastic. The chair's main character is defined by its back and armrest in colorful polypropylene molding.

Der Sessel Monza besteht aus einer Kombination von Kunststoff und Holz. Die wichtigsten Elemente des Stuhl sind sein Rücken und die Armlehnen aus buntem gegossenem Polypropylen.

The B Chair is characterized by its X-shaped legs and its foldable seat, which allows horizontal stacking. The underside of the seat can either be laminated in colors or in aluminum.

Der B Chair unterscheidet sich durch seine X-förmigen Beine und den klappbaren Sitz, wodurch er horizontal gestapelt werden kann. Die Unterseite des Sitzes kann entweder mit farbigem Laminat oder mit Aluminium bedeckt werden.

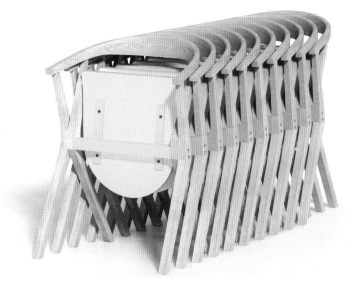

Myto is a cantilever chair, built as a monoblock with a supporting frame structure and a perforated seat and back. It is made entirely out of Ultradur High Speed plastic in a variety of colors.

Myto ist ein freischwingender Stuhl, der als Monoblock mit einer stützenden Rahmenstruktur und einem gelochten Sitz und Rücken konzipiert wurde. Er ist komplett aus Ultradur thermoplastischem Kunststoff in einer Reihe von Farben hergestellt.

Diana is a series of sheet metal tables ranging from A to F. They are multi-functional and serve as a side table, notebook stand, reference library or any other use.

Diana ist eine Kollektion von Stahlblechtischen, die von A bis F reicht. Alle sind vielfältig verwendbar, z.B. als Beistelltische, Notenstütze, Referenzbibliothek uvm.

Crash is a generous and spaciousness armchair offering individuals a place to "crash out" and relax. It consists of a tubular frame and a five-centimeter loose foam molded cover.

Crash ist ein großzügiger und geräumiger Sessel, der genug Platz zum Entspannen bietet. Er besteht aus einem Rohrrahmen und einem ca. 5 cm dicken lockeren, schaumgeformten Überzug.

As its name implies, 360°chair swivels around
and allows the users to sit in all directions. It
encourages dynamic sitting, short term and moving around.

Wie schon der Name andeutet, ist der Stuhl 360°
frei drehbar und erlaubt es Nutzern, beim Sitzen in
alle Richtungen zu blicken. Er unterstützt dynamisches Sitzen in Intervallen und mit Bewegung.

The Stool One barstool aluminum construction
highlights the stark, geometric pattern carved into
the angular seat. The lightweight stools can easily
be stacked.

Die Aluminiumstruktur des Barhockers One hebt
die streng geometrischen Muster, die in den ecki-
gen Sitz geschnitzt sind, hervor. Die Leichtgewich-
te sind einfach zu stapeln.

The Waver chair is reminiscent of a paraglider. Its
seat is made from high-tech fabric used for sports
equipment, which is hooked over the tubular
frame like a hammock.

Der Stuhl Waver ähnelt einem Gleitschirm. Sein
Sitz besteht aus einem High -Tech-Stoff, der übli-
cherweise für Sportgeräte benutzt wird, und ist an
dem Rohrrahmen wie eine Hängematte angehängt.

The Flow Armchair is a series of small armchairs whose carefully molded shells balance on different frames. These include four wooden legs, a metal pedestal, a tubular steel "sled" base, or wheels.

Der Flow Armchair ist eine Kollektion von kleinen Sesseln, deren sorgfältig geformte Schalen auf verschiedenen Untergestellen balancieren. Zu diesen gehören vier Holzbeine, ein Metallpodest, ein Schlitten-Stahlrohruntergestell und Räder.

Jean-Marie
Massaud

Jean-Marie Massaud (born in 1966, in Toulouse) is a French architect and designer. In 1990, he graduated from Les Ateliers, École Nationale Supérieure de Création Industrielle in Paris, where he soon created his own studio for industrial and interior design. His clients have included Yves Saint Laurent, Renault, B&B Italia, Cappellini and Magis, and he has created furniture, household products, and industrial equipment with equal skill and creativity. He has also worked in architecture, with projects in Japan and Mexico, as well as brand development. His approach to all these different fields is fluid, and resistant to trends and fashions. The quest, for Massaud, is constant, independent innovation. He has received a number of awards, including "Designer of the Year" at the the 2007 Salon du Meuble in Paris and the prestigious Italian Compasso d'Oro. His work is featured in the permanent collections of the Musée National d'Art Moderne and the Musée des Arts Décoratifs in Paris, as well as the Museum für Gestaltung in Zurich.

Jean-Marie Massaud (geb. 1966 in Toulouse) ist ein französischer Architekt und Designer. 1990 schloss er sein Studium an der Les Ateliers, École Nationale Supérieure de Création Industrielle in Paris ab und gründete bald darauf sein eigenes Studio für Industriedesign und Innenarchitektur. Zu seinen Kunden gehören unter anderem Yves Saint Laurent, Renault, B&B Italia, Cappellini und Magis, für die er Möbel, Haushaltsartikel und industrielles Werkzeug mit gleichbleibender Kunstfertigkeit und Kreativität entwirft. Er realisierte auch architektonische Projekte in Japan und Mexiko und arbeitete in der Markenentwicklung.

Im Umgang mit diesen verschiedenen Arbeitsbereichen hat er einen fließenden Stil, der resistent gegen Trends und Moden ist. Massauds Bestreben ist die konstant unabhängige Innovation. Er erhielt eine Reihe von Auszeichnungen, unter anderem 2007 den „Designer of the Year" bei dem Salon du Meuble in Paris und den angesehenen italienischen Compasso d'Oro.

Sein Werk befindet sich in der ständigen Sammlung des Musée National d'Art Moderne und dem Musée des Arts Décoratifs in Paris sowie dem Museum für Gestaltung in Zürich.

Terminal 1 is both a daybed and an armchair, whose fluid, amorphous plastic body that rests on a metallic frame. The expansive, sleek form perfectly balances angles and curves.

Terminal 1 ist gleichzeitig eine Schlafcouch und ein Sessel, dessen fließender amorpher Kunststoffkörper auf einem Metallrahmen ruht.

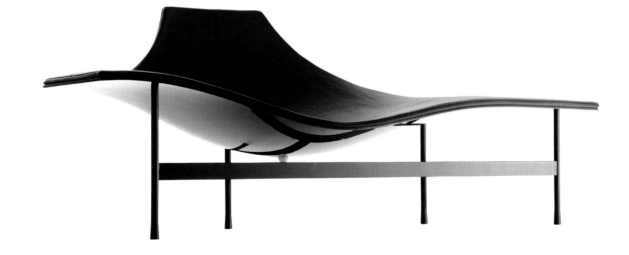

The Ad Hoc Armchair's intricate, hand-made brass structure differs slightly in each piece. The base is a rectangular prism of negative space, into which the shell is either carved or suspended.

Die aufwändige handgefertigte Messingstruktur des Stuhles Ad Hoc ist von Stück zu Stück leicht unterschiedlich. Das Untergestell ist ein recht-eckiges Prisma von negativem Raum, in welches die Schale entweder herausgearbeitet oder eingehängt ist.

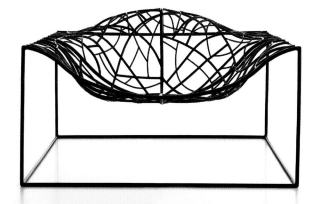

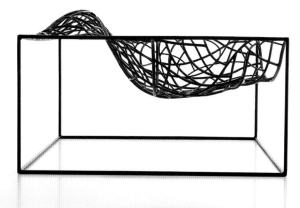

Synapsis is either a coffee table or a dining table, whose main feature is the steel rod structure that forms the base. Instead of ordinary table legs, the rods are intertwined into abstract pillars.

Synapsis ist als Couch- oder Esstisch erhältlich, dessen Hauptmerkmal die Stabstahlstruktur des Untergestelles ist. Anstatt normaler Tischbeine sind die Stäbe ineinander verschlungen, woraus abstrakte Säulenformen entstehen.

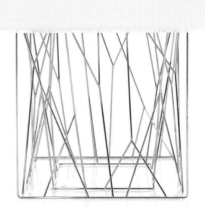

The Archibald Armchair is an elegant leather arm-chair whose thick shell rests on four short, thin metal legs. The simple form draws attention to the fold details in the backrest and over the arms.

The Sessel Archibald Armchair ist ein eleganter Ledersessel, dessen dicke Schale auf vier kurzen und dünnen Metallbeinen ruht. Die schlichte Form lenkt die Aufmerksamkeit auf die Details der Falten im Rückenteil und über den Armen.

Aster X is a new take on the classic film director chair, with the X-shaped frame supporting a heavier, more padded seat.

Aster X ist eine moderne Interpretation des klassischen Regisseurstuhls, wobei der X-förmige Rahmen einen schwereren gepolsterten Sitz trägt.

The Aspen Sofa is one long sweeping curve, like a ski slope, as the backrest tapers down to a stop. Two sofas can be joined back-to-back.

Das Sofa Aspen besteht aus einer langgezogenen gebogenen Kurve, ähnlich einer Skipiste, in der die Rückenlehne sich kontinuierlich verjüngt bis sie ihr Ende erreicht. Dadurch können zwei Sofas Rücken an Rücken gestellt werden.

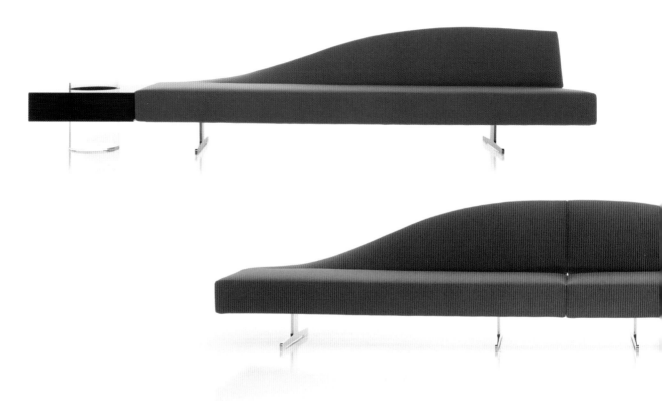

The Outline Chaise Longue rests on a rectangular steel base, and the seat dips down into the space below. The brightly coloured upholstery contrasts vividly with the visually light design.

Die Chaiselongue Outline sitzt auf einem rechteckigen Stahl-Untergestell mit einem Sitz, der sich abwärts in den unterliegenden Raum neigt. Die bunten Polster bilden einen lebhaften Kontrast zu dem optisch hellen Design.

*Arch Sofa balances on an improbably thin frame.
The wide and thickly upholstered body of the sofa
hangs calmly on an aluminum structure that is
only eight milimeters thick.*

*Das Sofa Arch balanciert auf einem extrem
dünnen Rahmen. Der breite und dick gepolsterte
Korpus des Sofas hängt ruhig auf einer Aluminiumstruktur, die nur acht Millimeter dick ist.*

The distinctive Wallace Armchair consists of a
shell of molded polyurethane on an irregular
metal base. The shell is covered with oversized
leather upholstery, which hangs off the edges of
the forms.

Der unverwechselbare Sessel Wallace besteht
aus einer Schale aus geformtem Polyurethan auf
einem ungleichmäßigen Metalluntergestell. Die
Schale ist mit überdimensionalen Lederpolstern
bedeckt, die über den Rand der Form hängen.

Woodstock is a simple coffee table made up of five long block of wood. These are painted and irregularly arranged, leaving the geometry of the design to speak for itself.

Woodstock ist ein puristischer Couchtisch, der aus fünf langen Holzblöcken besteht. Diese sind lackiert und unregelmäßig angeordnet, wodurch die Geometrie des Designs für sich selbst spricht.

Achille's metal frame is padded with foam and
upholstered in fabric, a process which both soft-
ens its lines, and makes the form solid and clear.

Der Metallrahmen von Achille ist mit Schaumstoff
gepolstert und mit Stoff bezogen. Dadurch werden
die Linien weicher, während die Form gefestigt und
klar erkennbar wird.

The Aston chairs are equally at home in the office
or in the living room. The graceful harmony of
echoed shapes in the backrest, seat, and armrests
make it stand out in any setting.

Die Stühle Aston passen genauso in ein Büro wie
in ein Wohnzimmer. Die anmutige Harmonie der
Formen von Rückenlehne, Sitz und Armlehnen
zieht die Blicke in allen Umgebungen auf sich.

Sean Sofa's clear geometric forms are repeated throughout the different components, but then tempered with soft materials, which take the edge off the contours.

Die klaren geometrischen Formen des Sofas Sean wiederholen sich in den verschiedenen Komponenten. Die Kombination mit weichen Stoffen mildert die Konturen ab.

The Kennedee Sofa is a modular sofa system that can be arranged at different angles and opened up in different directions. The indent details in the upholstery add an ornate element to the design.

Das Sofa Kennedee ist ein modulares Sofasystem das in verschiedenen Winkeln aufgestellt werden kann und das sich in verschiedene Richtungen öffnet. Die Einkerbungen in den Polstern fügen der Form eine kunstvoll verzierte Note hinzu.

The Joco Side Table is a minimalist black table whose delicate aesthetic belies its structural sturdiness. The thin tabletop is available in two different lengths.

Der Beistelltisch Joco ist ein minimalistischer schwarzer Tisch dessen grazile Ästhetik seine strukturelle Robustheit verbirgt. Die dünne Tisch-platte ist in zwei verschiedenen Längen erhältlich.

EOOS

EOOS is an Austrian design team formed by Gernot Bohmann (born 1968), Harald Gründl (born 1967) and Martin Bergmann (born 1963). The trio studied at the University of Applied Arts in Vienna, and founded EOOS in 1995. The studio specializes in furniture and product design as well as shop design. Their clients and collaborators include Adidas, Giorgio Armani, Matteograssi and Walter Knoll. EOOS describe their approach to design as „Poetical Analysis," suggesting that good design has artistic and cultural merit beyond its functional applications. This means that they do not simply approach the subject matter at face value, but instead they look for a deeper theme, and search for intuitive images, myths or rituals that the subject might evoke. This broader, more humanist perspective has won them

more than 50 international design prizes, icluding the Compasso d'Oro for the "Kube" conference seating system in 2004. "Kube" is typical of EOOS design in that the task at hand was expanded upon with creative and clever references, this time to the past – the seating system is reminiscent of the rows of seats in a Roman amphitheater, lending an air of antiquity and history to a modern conference room.

EOOS ist ein österreichisches Designer-team, gegründet von Gernot Bohmann (geb. 1968), Harald Gründl (geb. 1967) und Martin Bergmann (geb. 1963). Das Trio studierte an der Universität für angewandte Kunst in Wien und gründete EOOS im Jahr 1995. Das Studio ist auf Möbel- und Produktdesign so-wie Ladengestaltung spezialisiert. Zu seinen Kunden und Partnern gehören die Firmen Adidas, Giorgio Armani, Matteograssi und Walter Knoll.

EOOS beschreiben ihren Design-Ansatz als „Poetische Analyse", womit ausgedrückt werden soll, dass gutes Design einen künst-lerischen und kulturellen Wert besitzt, der über seine rein funktionelle Anwendung hi-nausgeht. In der Praxis bedeutet dies, dass EOOS nicht einfach nur das Augenscheinli-che der Dinge betrachtet, sondern stattdes-sen ein tieferes Thema und intuitive Bilder, Mythen oder Rituale, die das Objekt hervor-ruft, erforscht.

Dieser expansivere, menschlichere An-satz hat den drei Designern mehr als 450 internationale Designauszeichnungen be-schert, unter anderem den Compasso d'Oro im Jahr 2004 für das Konferenzsitzmöbelsys-tem „Kube". Dieses ist ein typisches EOOS-Design, in dem die eigentliche Aufgabe durch kreative und raffinierte Referenzen erweitert wurde – diesmal mit Bezug zur Vergangen-heit, denn das Sitzsystem erinnert an die Sitzreihen in einem römischen Amphithea-ter, wodurch modernen Konferenzräumen ein Anstrich von Antike und Geschichte ver-liehen wird.

The Cuoio Lounge is an elegant and minimalist lounge chair available with or without armrests, and which has a matching ottoman. The chair has a frame in steel and a seat in leather.

Der Cuoio Lounge ist ein eleganter und mini-malistischer Klubsessel den es mit oder ohne Armlehnen gibt und der mit einem passenden Polsterhocker ergänzt wird. Der Sessel hat einen Stahlrahmen und Lederpolsterung.

The Jaan Armchair and Sofa are a combination of living and office furniture. The compact cube crowns the high, elegant legs in a balanced harmony of lightness and weight.

Der Sessel und das Sofa Jaan bieten eine Kombination von Wohn- und Büromöbel. Der kompakte Würfel krönt die hohen eleganten Beine mit einer ausgeglichenen Harmonie von Leichtigkeit und Schwere.

The Jason 390 sofa has an armrest extension mechanism hidden within the frame. The legs come in different chrome finishes, with upholstery in leather.

Das Sofa Jason 390 hat eine Ausfahrfunktion für die Armlehnen in seinem Rahmen versteckt. Die Beine des Sofas sind in verschieden Chromvariationen erhältlich und es hat einen Lederbezug.

There are 28 different models of the minimalist, stackable Jason Lite chair. They vary in width, and in the design of the armrests and backs.

Es gibt 28 verschiedene Modelle des minimalistischen stapelbaren Stuhls Jason Lite. Sie haben verschiedene Breiten sowie Arm- und Rückenlehnen.

The Andoo Lounge Chair's rigid hardwood frame is upholstered in soft leather, and it comes with a high or low back, with or without armrests, and with an optional foot stool.

Der steife Hartholzrahmen des Klubsessels Andoo ist mit weichem Leder gepolstert. Es gibt ihn mit hohem oder niedrigem Rücken, mit oder ohne Armlehnen und wahlweise mit einem Fußschemel.

Delicate trelliswork supports the round glass top
of the Oota Table. It is perfect as a coffee table
and is available in three different sizes, with
black-coated or stainless steel polished framework.

*Zartes Gitterwerk stützt die runde Glasplatte des
Tischs Oota. Er ist perfekt geeignet als Couchtisch
und in drei verschiedenen Größen erhältlich,
jede mit einem Hochglanzrahmen der entweder
schwarz lackiert oder aus rostfreiem Stahl ist.*

Living Landscape 750 is a range of sofas that incorporates the room it stands in. Integrated shelves, round tables and round footstools complete the range.

Living Landscape 750 ist eine Sofa Kollektion die den Raum in dem sie steht einbezieht. Integrierte Regale, runde Tische und runde Hocker ergänzen die Reihe.

Thanks to one of EOOS's own patented mechanisms, the Living Platform can be easily transformed from a sofa into a daybed.

Dank einem Mechanismus der von EOOS patentiert wurde, kann die Living Platform sehr einfach von einem Sofa zu einem Bett verwandelt werden.

Kube is a seating system for conference rooms or public events. The seats can be folded up and down and their backs feature folding tables and lighting and audio equipment.

Kube ist ein Sitzmöbelsystem für Konferenzräume. Die Sitze können zusammen- und hochgeklappt werden und auf ihrer Rückseite befinden sich Klapptische sowie Leuchtmittel und audiovisuelle Geräte.

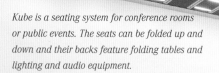

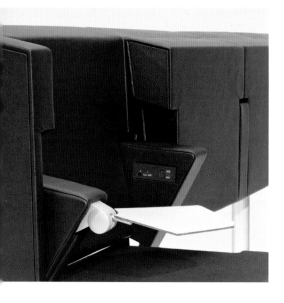

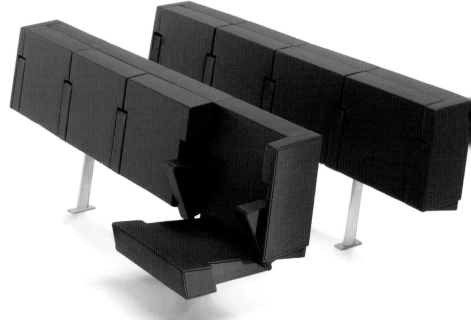

The sturdy tabletop of Tadeo rests on the recessed base. The table comes in different variants with and without EOOS's special extending mechanism.

Die stabile Tischplatte von Tadeo ruht auf dem zurückgesetzten Untergestell. Der Tisch ist in verschiedenen Variationen erhältlich mit und ohne dem speziell von EOOS entwickelten Hubmechanismus.

ST04 Backenzahn, which means "molar", is a tooth-shaped stool or side table carved out of solid wood. Four identical pieces are joined together, and slight gaps remain to distinguish them.

ST04 Backenzahn, ist ein zahnförmiger Hocker oder Beistelltisch aus massivem Holz. Vier identische Teile werden zusammengefügt und durch Schattenfugen voneinander getrennt.

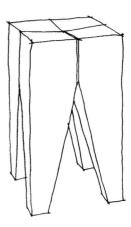

Philipp Mainzer

Philipp Mainzer (born in 1969 in Hamburg) is a German architect and designer, and the current managing and creative director of e15. Mainzer completed his education in England, studying product design at Central Saint Martins University, then architecture at the Architectural Association University in London. In 1995, he and Florian Asche founded the design company e15 in London, which has since gone on to gain international recognition for its furniture, all of which is manufactured in Germany, as well as its interior design and architectural services. Mainzer oversees all aspect of e15's activities, and has also been very successful with his own designs. The "Bigfoot" table, with solid wood legs carved out of the center of a tree, leaving the annual rings visible, has become an iconic piece for e15. In 2007, he was awarded the German Design Award for the "Shiraz" sofa system, which was inspired both by traditional Persian sofas and the design of Western hotel lobbies. The result is a flexible, modular seating system. Each module is composed of a base, which comes with or without a backrest, and an oversized cushion that forms the seat. These pieces can be exchanged, combined, and arranged in a number of different ways, creating different solutions for different environments. Since 2009, Mainzer has also been a member of the German Design Council.

Philipp Mainzer (geboren 1969 in Hamburg) ist ein deutscher Architekt und Designer, der als geschäftsführender Gesellschafter und Kreativ-Direktor von e15 tätig ist.

Mainzer studierte in England Produktdesign an der Central Saint Martins University und Architektur an der Architectural Association University in London. Im Jahr 1995 gründeten er und Florian Asche das Designbüro e15 in London, welches internationale Erfolge mit seinen Möbeln „made in Germany" sowie mit Leistungen im Bereich Innenarchitektur und Architektur erzielt. Mainzer beaufsichtigt alle Aktivitäten von e15 und entwirft außerdem noch sehr erfolgreich eigene Produkte. Der Tisch „Bigfoot" z. B. ist mit seinen massiven Holzbeinen, die aus dem Kern eines Baumes gefertigt werden, wobei die Jahresringe sichtbar bleiben, ein Markenzeichen mit Kultstatus für e15. Mainzer erhielt 2007 den anerkannten Designpreis Deutschland für den Entwurf des Sofa-Systems „Shiraz", welches von traditionellen persischen Sitzmöbeln sowie den Möbeln klassischer westlicher Hotellobbys inspiriert wurde. Das Ergebnis ist ein flexibles modulares System aus Sitzelementen. Jedes Element besteht aus dem Sitz mit oder ohne Rückenteil sowie einem übergroßen Kissen, welches die Sitzauflage bildet. Diese Elemente können ausgetauscht, kombiniert und auf verschiedene Arten angeordnet werden und bieten somit verschiedene Lösungen für unterschiedliche Situationen. Seit 2009 ist Mainzer auch Präsidiumsmitglied des Rats für Formgebung (German Design Council).

TA04 Bigfoot is a massive wooden table whose four legs each include the center of the tree, leaving the annual rings visible at their tops.

TA04 Bigfoot ist ein Massivholztisch, dessen vier Beine jeweils aus dem Kern eines Baumes gefertigt wurden, wobei die Jahresringe oben sichtbar bleiben.

The main module of the SF02 Kashan is a wide
seat with a solid wood headboard. Using notches,
the headboard can be attached to a long side
frame, forming the start of a sofa.

Das Hauptelement des SF02 Kashan ist ein breiter
Sitz mit einem Massivholz-Kopfende. Durch spe-
zielle Kerben kann das Kopfende an einem langen
Seitenrahmen befestigt werden um den Anfang
eines Sofas zu bilden.

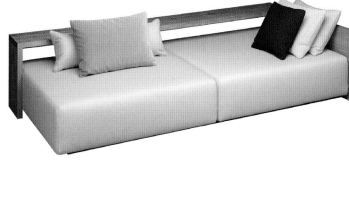

SF03 Shiraz was inspired by traditional Persian seating designs. The central piece is the individual seating "island", to which different backrests can be added.

SF03 Shiraz ist von traditionellen persischen Sitzmöbeldesigns inspiriert. Das Kernstück ist die individuelle „Sitzinsel" an welche diverse Rücken-lehnen hinzugefügt werden können.

The CM05 Habibi tables were also inspired by the Middle East, this time by traditional tea services. The delicate metal tables, which consists of trays perched on slender legs, are polished by hand.

Die Tische CM05 Habibi sind auch vom Nahen Osten inspiriert, in diesem Fall von traditionellen Teeservices. Die zierlichen Metalltische, die aus Tabletts auf schlanken Beinen bestehen, sind von Hand poliert.

SL02 MO's heavy wooden frame has a shallow recess for the mattres, and a central bracket for additional strength. The clean lines of the minimalist design are left uninterrupted.

Der schwere Holzrahmen von SL02 MO hat eine flache Mulde für die Matratze und einen zentralen Träger für zusätzliche Tragkraft. Die klaren Linien des minimalistischen Designs bleiben hiervon unberührt.

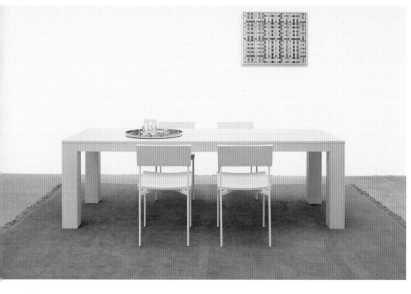

TA17 London's legs are wide but not thick, changing the view of the table from different angles. The top is cradled within them, leaving them entirely visible and exposing the construction concept.

Die Beine des TA17 London's sind zwar breit, aber nicht dick, wodurch der Tisch je nach Blickwinkel immer wieder anders erscheint. Die Tischplatte ist in die Beine versenkt, wodurch diese sichtbar bleiben und das Konstruktionsprinzip verdeutlichen.

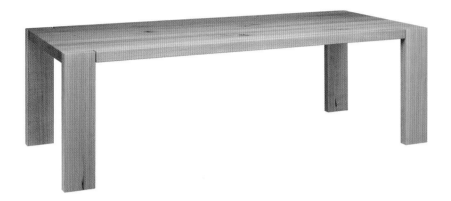

TA15 Jack is similar Bigfoot, but this time the focus is entirely on the proportions. The thinner tabletop highlights the thick legs, and the optional white paint makes the form stand out even more.

TA15 Jack ähnelt Bigfoot, aber diesmal ist der eindeutige Schwerpunkt auf den Proportionen. Die dünnere Tischplatte hebt die starken Beine hervor, während die wahlweise weiße Farbe die Form noch stärker betont.

The aptly named Steelwood armchair is made from a daring combination of wood and steel. The chair will change appearance as the materials age and a patina forms.

Der Stuhl mit dem treffenden Namen Steelwood Chair ist aus einer eleganten Kombination von Stahl und Holz hergestellt. Sein Aussehen wird sich über die Zeit hin verändern, wenn das Material altert und eine Patina entsteht.

Ronan & Erwan
Bouroullec

Ronan and Erwan Bouroullec (born in 1971 and 1976, respectively, in Quimper) are a French design team. Initially, Ronan worked alone, but soon was assisted by his younger brother Erwan, even as he was still a student at the École des Beaux-Arts at Cergy-Pontoise, and the two brothers became a team in 1999. Their products are the result of a constant dialogue, as they often start out with different visions and different viewpoints. By the end of the design process, it is impossible to attribute any one aspect of the piece to either brother. In 2000, they were commissioned to design an entire shop in Paris for Issey Miyake, and in 2002 they began working on the "Joyn" office system for Vitra. The system was designed with collaboration in mind. The large tabletop and generous proportions, which were inspired by the

large kitchen tables of farmhouses around which domestic life revolved, foster a sense of communal space. The same year, they were named "Creator of the Year" at the Salon du Meuble in Paris. Their creations have been shown at museums and exhibits around the world, and they are featured in the permanent exhibits of Centre Pompidou in Paris and the London Design Museum. Both brothers also teach: they regularly take part in worskhops and seminars in design schools around Europe, and Ronan is a professor at the École Cantonale d'Art de Lausanne in Switzerland.

Ronan and Erwan Bouroullec (geboren 1971 und 1976 in Quimper) sind ein französisches Designteam. Ronan arbeitete zunächst allein, wurde aber bald von seinem jüngeren Bruder Erwan noch während dessen Studienzeit an der École des Beaux-Arts in Cergy-Pontoise unterstützt. Ihre Produkte entstehen aus einem ständigen Dialogprozess, da sie oft mit unterschiedlichen Visionen und Ansätzen an Projekte herangehen. Am Ende des Designprozesses aber ist es unmöglich, einen bestimmten Aspekt eines Stückes einem der Brüder zuzuordnen. Im Jahr 2000 erhielten sie den Auftrag einen gesamten Showroom für Issey Miyake in Paris zu gestalten und 2002 begannen sie die Arbeit an dem Bürosystem „Joyn" für Vitra. Das System wurde basierend auf dem Gedanken der Zusammenarbeit konzipiert. Die große Tischplatte mit der großzügigen Fläche wurde von bäuerlichen Küchentischen, um die sich das häusliche Leben dreht, inspiriert; dadurch sollte das Gefühl eines gemeinsamen Raumes erweckt werden.

Im gleichen Jahr erhielten sie den Titel „Creator of the Year" bei dem Salon du Meuble in Paris. Ihre Arbeiten wurden in Museen und Ausstellungen rund um die Welt gezeigt und sie gehören zu den ständigen Sammlungen des Centre Pompidou in Paris und dem London Design Museum. Beide Brüder sind auch in der Lehre tätig; sie nehmen regelmäßig als Experten an Workshops und Seminaren von europäischen Designschulen teil. Ronan ist außerdem Professor an der École Cantonale d'Art de Lausanne in der Schweiz.

The Algues are a surprising interior design piece based on molded plastic modules. These can be used to create screens or partitions with a dreamy underwater aesthetic.

Die Algues sind ein überraschendes innenarchi-tektonisches Element, das auf gegossenen Plastik-bausteinen basiert. Diese können als Abschirmung oder Raumteiler mit einer verträumten Unterwas-ser - Ästhetik verwendet werden.

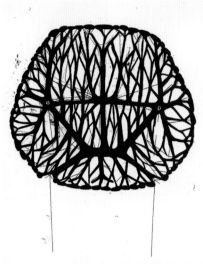

The Vegetal chair looks as if it developed organically. The seat is woven out of plastic branches, and supported by ribs that grow out from the legs. All that is missing are the leaves.

Der Stuhl Vegetal sieht aus, als sei er aus organischem Material gewachsen. Der Sitz ist aus Plastik-Ästen gewoben und wird von Rippen gestützt, die aus den Beinen hervor wachsen. Das Einzige, was fehlt, sind die Blätter.

The Slow Chair is an experiment with knitted textiles. Stretched over a metal frame, the translucent fabric cover is surprisingly strong, and subtly moulds itself to the shape of the sitter's body.

Der Stuhl Slow ist ein Experiment aus gestrickten Textilien. Über einen Metallrahmen gezogen, ist der durchsichtige Stoffbezug überraschend stark und verformt sich fast unmerklich, um sich dem Körper des Sitzenden anzupassen.

The Spring Chair balances on an impossibly thin metal base, and the spring-mounted footrest responds to the slightest movement. The result is a light, almost delicate take on the classic recliner.

Der Stuhl Spring balanciert auf einer außergewöhnlich dünnen Metallstruktur, während die gefederte Fußstütze auf die kleinste Bewegung reagiert. Das Resultat ist eine leichte, fast zerbrechliche Version eines klassischen Lehnstuhls.

The Striped Chair collection repurposes the tubular steel frame to create a minimal and coherent range of outdoor furniture. Each piece is composed only of polyamide strips fitted onto metal frames.

Bei der Kollektion Striped Chair wird der Stahlrohrrahmen für eine minimalistische und zusammenhängende Reihe von Möbeln für den Außenbereich wiederverwendet. Jedes Stück besteht nur aus Polyamid-Streifen, die an Metallrahmen befestigt sind.

The Alcove series creates a room within the room. The unusually high backrests and side panels provide comfort and privacy, perfect for relaxing or retiring from the world outside.

Mit der Serie Alcove werden Räume innerhalb von Räumen geschaffen. Die ungewöhnlich hohen Rückenlehnen und Seitenwände bieten Komfort und eine Privatsphäre, die perfekt geeignet ist, um sich zu entspannen und sich von der Welt zurückzuziehen.

The Joyn system was the Bouroullecs' first foray into office furniture. The idea was to create a flexible, adaptable workspace that encourages collaboration and communication.

Das System Joyn war der erste Ausflug der Bouroullecs in die Welt der Büromöbel. Die Grundidee war ein flexibler, anpassungsfähiger Arbeitsplatz, der die Zusammenarbeit und Kommunikation fördert.

The Softshell Chair earns its name thanks to its curved, organic lines and comfortable shell. This flexible chair is height-adjustable and can be upholstered in either leather or fabric.

Der Stuhl Softshell Chair verdankt seinen Namen den kurvenförmigen, organischen Linien und der bequemen Hülle. Die Höhe dieses flexiblen Stuhls kann beliebig eingestellt werden; er ist sowohl mit einem Leder- als auch mit einem Stoffbezug erhältlich.

The Worknest Chair is a cozy take on the traditional office chair. The soft, fabric cover and the calm, ergonomic shape reflects the brothers' emphasis on designs created for humans, not machines.

Der Stuhl Worknest ist eine gemütliche Variante des traditionellen Bürostuhls. Der weiche Stoffbezug und die ruhige, ergonomische Form verdeutlichen die Absicht der Brüder, Möbel für Menschen und nicht für Maschinen zu entwerfen.

The Playns office system allows open, collaborative spaces to be grouped into different "islands" as needed, so that each user or office can set up their workspace to suit their individual needs.

Mit dem Bürosystem Playns können offene gemeinschaftliche Räume geschaffen werden, die je nach Bedarf in verschiedene „Inseln" aufgeteilt werden. Nutzer oder Bürogemeinschaften können so ihren Arbeitsplatz nach ihren eigenen Bedürfnissen gestalten.

Designed in collaboration with Christophe de la Fontaine, the Bent series includes an armchair and a side table. Laser-cut aluminum sheets, bent into shape, emphasize the highly geometric forms.

In Zusammenarbeit mit Christophe de la Fontaine entwickelt, gehören zu der Serie Bent ein Sessel und ein Beistelltisch. Lasergeschnittene Aluminiumbleche, die in Form gebogen sind, unterstreichen die stark geometrischen Formen.

Stefan Diez

Stefan Diez (born in 1971 in Freising) is a German designer. His meteoric rise to success started with a three-year apprenticeship as a carpenter and a year spent working in India, before going on to study industrial design at the Academy of Fine Arts in Stuttgart. In 2003, after briefly working for the German designer Konstantin Grcic, Diez founded his own design studio in Munich. He has since worked in both product and exhibition design, creating furniture, tableware, and exhibition installations for companies such as Moroso, Thonet, e15, and Wilkhahn. When designing furniture, Diez takes particular interest in his chosen material and the technology used to create the piece, and he is equally adept working with wood, leather, metal and plastic, lending a remarkable diversity to his projects. The "404" stool, for example, is made entirely out of wood. No screws or joints are used to assemble the chairs, instead, the parts are joined using only grooves and glue. The form is typically minimalist, but with an innovative twist – the wooden seat is improbably bent into an abstract shape reminiscent of a saddle. Diez's work has already earned him widespread recognition and a number of prizes, including the Design Award of the Federal Republic of Germany in 2006 for silverware.

Stefan Diez (geb. 1971 in Freising) ist ein deutscher Designer. Sein kometenhafter Erfolg begann nach seiner dreijährigen Schreinerlehre und einem Jahr in Indien. Danach studierte er Industriedesign an der Stuttgarter Akademie der Bildenden Künste. Im Jahr 2003, nachdem er kurze Zeit für den deutschen Designer Konstantin Grcic gearbeitet hatte, gründete er sein eigenes Designstudio in München. Dort entwickelt er Produkte wie Möbel, Geschirr und Ausstellungskonzepte für Firmen wie Moroso, Thonet, e15, und Wilkhahn.

In seinen Möbeldesigns legt Diez besonderen Wert auf das ausgewählte Material und die angewandte Technologie. Er ist gleichermaßen bewandert in der Arbeit mit Holz, Leder, Metall und Plastik, was seine Projekte außergewöhnlich vielseitig macht. Der Hocker „404" z.B. ist komplett aus Holz gefertigt. Es wurden keine Schrauben verwendet um die Stühle der Serie zusammenzusetzen; stattdessen sind die Teile nur mit Fugen und Leim zusammengefügt. Die Form ist typisch minimalistisch, aber mit einem innovativen Touch – die hölzerne Sitzfläche wurde zu einer amorphen, fließenden Form gebogen, die einem Sattel ähnelt.

Diez hat schon viele Auszeichnungen und Preise für seine Arbeiten gewonnen, unter anderem den Designpreis der Bundesrepublik Deutschland in Silber für sein für die Firma Thomas gestaltetes Oven-to-table (feuerfestes Geschirr) Programm.

The CH04 Houdini armchair and side chair use bent sheets of plywood to create two shells for the seat and the backrests. The result is a clear silhouette whose underlying structure almost disappears.

Für den Sessel und Stuhl CH04 Houdini wurden gebogene Sperrholzplatten als zwei Schalen für Rücken und Sitzfläche verwendet. Das Resultat ist eine klare Silhouette, deren Unterstruktur fast unsichtbar ist.

The EC03 Eugene chair is similar to the Houdini series in its plywood construction, but the shell has been widened and deepened to create a more relaxed lounge chair.

Der Stuhl EC03 Eugene hat eine ähnliche Sperr-holzkonstruktion wie die der Houdini -Serie, aber die Schale wurde verbreitert und vertieft, um einen mehr entspannten Klubsessel zu schaffen.

The EC02 Bessy lounge chair has the same high back as Eugene, but with the addition of a wide, round seat, which is comfortably upholstered. The seat is also available without the backrest, as a stool.

Der Klubsessel EC02 Bessy hat den gleichen ho-hen Rücken wie der Eugene, aber zusätzlich eine weite, runde, komfortabel gepolsterte Sitzfläche. Der gleiche Sessel ist auch ohne Rückenlehne als Hocker erhältlich.

*The Bess sofa is Bessie's more imposing counter-
part. Expanded to seat two people, the round,
upholstered seat is now an oblong, and the graceful plywood backrest is equally elongated.*

*Das Sofa Bess ist die monumentalere Version von
Bessie. Erweitert zu einem Zweisitzer, sind sowohl
die runde gepolsterte Sitzfläche als auch die grazi-
öse Sperrholzrückenlehne nun langgezogen oval.*

*Modular and stackable, New Order is a versatile
piece. The simple, industrial metal frame can be
fitted with a range of accessories, including doors,
dividers, and works as a shelf and as a partition.*

*Modular und stapelbar ist New Order ein vielseiti-
ges Möbelstück. Der einfache industrielle Metallrahmen kann durch eine Reihe von Accessoires,
wie z.B. Türen und Trennwände, ergänzt und als
Regal oder Raumteiler verwendet werden.*

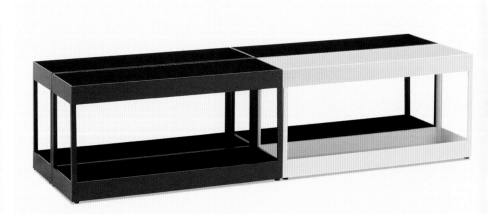

The Jean barstool also evolved from the Houdini chair, this time with long, thin legs and a simple seat. A horizontal bar is added for stability, and the stool is available in several cheery colors.

Der Barhocker Jean ist ebenfalls eine Weiterentwicklung des Stuhles Houdini, diesmal mit langen dünnen Beinen und einer einfachen Sitzfläche. Eine horizontale Stange wurde zur Stabilität hinzugefügt; der Hocker ist in vielen fröhlichen Farben erhältlich.

The remarkable 404 chair takes the classic bent plywood chair into a whole new direction. Fluid lines, a cantilevered backrest and an improbably curved seat distinguish the design.

Der ausgefallen wirkende Stuhl 404 gibt dem klassisch gebogenen Sperrholzstuhl eine völlig neue Richtung. Fließende Linien, eine freischwingende Rückenlehne und eine außergewöhnlich gebogene Sitzfläche zeichnen das Design aus.

In the 404H stool, the curved seat is inverted. The result is a curious form that is reminiscent of saddle, giving an extra creative flourish to an already dynamic piece.

Die gebogene Sitzfläche des Hockers 404H ist seitenverkehrt. Dies ergibt eine ausgefallene Form, die einem Sattel ähnelt und dem dynamischen Möbelstück einen zusätzlichen kreativen Anstrich gibt.

Chassis uses technology normally reserved for the automobile industry for its unique frame. One single piece of sheet steel is used to create the shell of the chair, then a detachable seat is added.

Für den einzigartigen Rahmen von Chassis wurden Technologien angewandt, die normalerweise der Automobil-Industrie vorbehalten sind. Ein einziges Stück Stahlblech wurde für die Sitzschale verwendet, auf die ein abnehmbarer Sitz befestigt wurde.

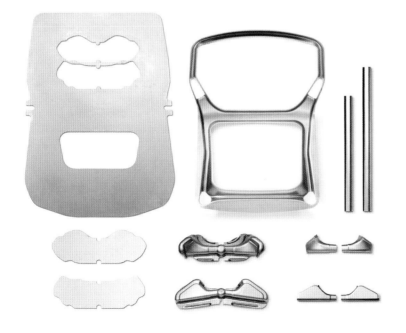

Dice is an innovative, modular storage program. Different fabric-covered elements, including cupboards, a sideboard, and accessories, including a mirror, can be arranged on a wall as users see fit.

Dice ist ein innovatives modulares Aufbewahrungsprogramm. Verschiedene mit Stoff bezogene Elemente wie Schränke, ein Sideboard und Zubehör (u.a. ein Spiegel) können an der Wand nach Belieben angebracht werden.

Upon is a wide-ranging family that includes a table, a coat rack, and bench. The unifiying element is the white, twisted sheet metal that forms the intriguing structures.

Upon ist ein weitläufiges Programm, zu dem ein Tisch, eine Garderobe und eine Bank gehören. Das verbindende Element ist das weiße, gebogene Stahlblech, aus dem die faszinierenden Strukturen gefertigt sind.

selected retailers

ausgewählte
Händler

Design-Werkstatt GmbH

Ostra-Allee 11, 01067 Dresden

T +49 (0)351 801 46 59

F +49 (0)351 801 46 57

info@designwerkstatt-dresden.de

minimumoffice gmbh

Helmholtzstraße 2–9, 10587 Berlin

T +49 (0)30 394 09 68 01

F +49 (0)30 394 09 68 19

info@minimumoffice.de

gärtner Internationale Möbel

Große Bleichen 23, 20354 Hamburg

T +49 (0)40 356 00 90

F +49 (0)40 35 60 09 39

info@gaertnermoebel.de

(smow) GmbH

Burgplatz 2, 04109 Leipzig

T +49 (0)341 124 83 30

F +49 (0)341 124 83 33

leipzig@smow.de

minimum einrichten gmbh

im stilwerk Kantstraße 17, 10623 Berlin

T +49 (0)30 31 99 85 00

F +49 (0)30 319 98 50 99

info@minimum.de

Seydlitz GmbH & Co. KG

Theaterstraße 15, 30159 Hannover

T +49 (0)511 270 70 70

F +49 (0)511 270 70 79

info@seydlitz.de

MachART Objekteinrichtungs GmbH

Moritzstraße 19, 09111 Chemnitz

T +49 (0)371 60 00 40

F +49 (0)371 600 04 10

info@machart-einrichtung.de

MODUS Möbel GmbH

Wielandstraße 27–28, 10707 Berlin

T +49 (0)30 889 15 60

F +49 (0)30 88 91 56 29

info@modus-moebel.de

loeser braunschweig gmbh

Gördelinger Straße 47, 38100 Braunschweig

T +49 (0)531 12 09 90

F +49 (0)531 120 99 20

info@loeser-braunschweig.de

citizenoffice GmbH

Speditionstrasse 17, 40221 Düsseldorf

T +49 (0)211 302 06 00

F +49 (0)211 30 20 60 20

info@citizenoffice.de

funktion gerhard wolf gmbh

Friedensplatz 8, 64283 Darmstadt

T +49 (0)651 78 07 80 10

F +49 (0)651 78 07 80 78

info@funktionmoebel.de

Fleiner Internationale Einrichtungen

Rosenbergstraße 106, 70193 Stuttgart

T +49 (0)711 635 00

F +49 (0)711 635 01 98

infoline@fleiner-moebel.de

Wim Gelhard GmbH Einrichtungsbedarf

Schliepstraße 12, 44135 Dortmund

T +49 (0)231 57 89 89

F +49 (0)231 52 97 97

www.wim-gelhard.de

Maurer Einrichtungen GmbH

Fürstenstraße 15, 66111 Saarbrücken

T +49 (0)681 58 26 28

F +49 (0)681 58 26 01

info@maurer-einrichtungen.de

Sommer Einrichtungen Gerhard Sommer

Alleenstraße 5, 71638 Ludwigsburg

T +49 (0)7141 960 60

F +49 (0)7141 90 30 32

sommer.einrichtungen@t-online.de

Hans Frick GmbH Inneneinrichtungen

Kaiserstraße 28, 60311 Frankfurt/Main

T +49 (0)69 28 51 31

F +49 (0)69 28 12 43

info@frick.de

Axel Walther Wohnbedarf GmbH

Gilgenstraße 26a, 67346 Speyer

T +49 (0)6232 752 67

F +49 (0)6232 265 71

info@axelwalther.de

Wohndesign Werner Enzmann GmbH

Eberhardstraße 15, 72764 Reutlingen

T +49 (0)7121 34 62 12

F +49 (0)7121 31 02 39

info@wohndesign-reutlingen.de

burger inneneinrichtung gmbh

Waldstraße 89–91, 76133 Karlsruhe

T +49 (0)721 91 32 20

F +49 (0)721 913 22 22

info@burger.de

Thalmeier-Einrichtungen GmbH

Marienplatz 1, 84405 Dorfen

T +49 (0)8081 936 70

F +49 (0)8081 93 67 29

einrichtungen@thalmeier.org

et sedia schadt und herramhof gmbh

Kreuzgasse 1, 93047 Regensburg

T +49 (0)941 59 56 90

F +49 (0)941 595 69 79

kontakt@etsedia.de

Welzer Wohnen

Kronenstraße 42, 78054 VS-Schwenningen

T +49 (0)7720 85 56 80

F +49 (0)7720 85 56 85

info@welzer-wohnen.de

Thalmeier-Einrichtungen GmbH

Haager Straße 10, 85435 Erding

T +49 (0)8122 959 84 30

F +49 (0)8122 959 84 31

erding@thalmeier.org

Teo Jakob AG

Gerechtigkeitsgasse 25, CH 3000 Bern 8

T +41 (0)31 327 57 00

F +41 (0)31 327 57 01

info@teojakob.ch

Seipp Wohnen GmbH

Bismarckstraße 35, 79761 Waldshut

T +49 (0)7751 83 60

F +49 (0)7751 836 90

wohnen@seipp.com

pfaehler einrichtung GmbH

Frauenstraße 9–11, 89073 Ulm

T +49 (0)731 650 27

F +49 (0)731 68 526

info@pfaehler-ulm.de

Thöny Wohnen Office Project

Bahnhofstrasse 16, FL-9494 Schaan

T +423 237 41 41

F +423 237 41 42

info@moebelthoeny.li

manufacturers
Hersteller

Alias
www.aliasdesign.it

Andreu World
www.andreuworld.com

Arper
www.arper.com

artek
www.artek.fi

Artifort
www.artifort.com

B&B ITALIA
www.bebitalia.it

BD Barcelona Design
www.bdbarcelona.com

BELUX
www.belux.com

Böwer
www.boewer.com

Caimi Brevetti
www.caimi.com

cappellini
www.cappellini.it

Carl Hansen & Son
www.carlhansen.com

Cassina
www.cassina.com

ClassiCon
www.classicon.com

De Padova
www.depadova.it

e15
www.e15.com

edra
www.edra.com

Established & Sons
www.establishedandsons.com

Fritz Hansen
www.fritzhansen.com

GLAS ITALIA
www.glasitalia.com

Herman Miller
www.hermanmiller.com

iittala
www.iittala.com

interlübke
www.interluebke.de

Knoll International
www.knoll-int.com

Lema
www.lemamobili.com

Ligne Roset
www.ligne-roset.de

Living Divani
www.livingdivani.it

Magis
www.magisdesign.com

matteograssi
www.matteograssi.it

MatzForm
www.matzform.com

MDF Italia
www.mdfitalia.it

Minotti
www.minotti.com

Nils Holger Moormann
www.moormann.de

Moroso
www.moroso.it

Pastoe
www.pastoe.com

PLANK
www.plank.it

Poliform
www.poliform.it

Poltrona Frau
www.poltronafrau.com

porro
www.porro.com

PP MØBLER
www.ppdk.com

Richard Lampert
www.richard-lampert.de

Schönbuch
www.schoenbuch.de

sdr+
www.sdr-plus.com

Swedese Möbler
www.swedese.se

THONET
www.thonet.de

USM Modular Furniture
www.usm.com

viccarbe
www.viccarbe.com

Vitra
www.vitra.com

VITSŒ
www.vitsoe.com

WALTER KNOLL
www.walterknoll.de

WILDE+SPIETH
www.wilde-spieth.de

Wilkhahn
www.wilkhahn.de

zanotta
www.zanotta.it

designers

Designer

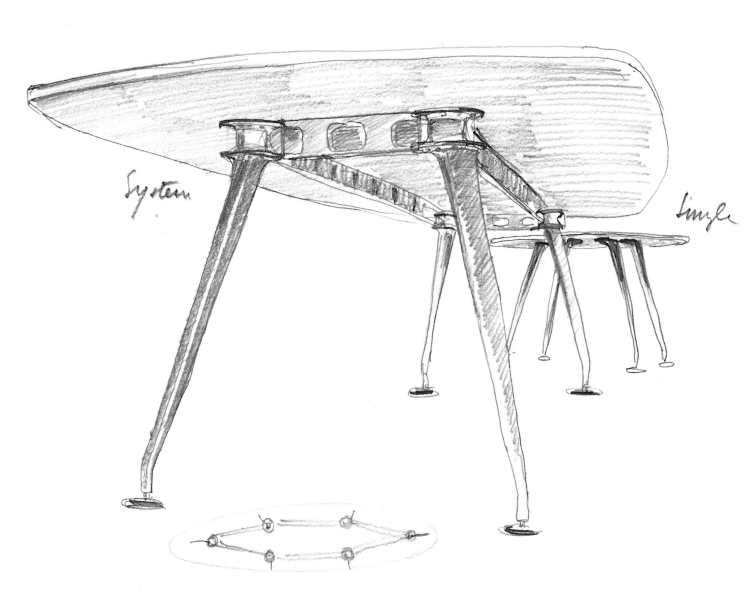

Alvar Aalto	030
Werner Aisslinger	262
Ron Arad	168
Mario Bellini	130
Harry Bertoia	090
Ronan & Erwan Bouroullec	310
Marcel Breuer	040
Fernando & Humberto Campana	174
Achille Castiglioni	094
Antonio Citterio	158
Le Corbusier	020
Stefan Diez	318
Rodolfo Dordoni	182
Charles and Ray Eames	068
Egon Eiermann	060
EOOS	290
Naoto Fukasawa	192
Eileen Gray	008
Konstantin Grcic	268
Fritz Haller & Paul Schärer	100
James Irvine	220
Arne Jacobsen	050
Hella Jongerius	258
Toshiyuki Kita	136
Poul Kjærholm	116
Axel Kufus	226
Lievore, Altherr, Molina	148
Piero Lissoni	202
Philipp Mainzer	302
Jean-Marie Massaud	278
Alberto Meda	142
Ludwig Mies van der Rohe	014
Jasper Morrison	232
Verner Panton	104
Pierre Paulin	108
Jean Prouvé	044
Dieter Rams	124
Eero Saarinen	078
Maarten Van Severen	216
Mart Stam	036
Patricia Urquiola	242
Hans J. Wegner	082

Picture Credit
Abbildungsnachweis

ADAGP, centre georges pompidou / MNAM-Cci/ Bibliothéque Kandinsky/ Fonds Cardot-Joly 45
courtesy of Alias 146 b., 147, 220, 222, 240 b., 241 b.
courtesy of Andreu World S.A. 150 b., 151, 153, 155
Archive of the publishing house 272 a.l., 272 m., 274 a., 274 b.l.
courtesy of Arper spa 149, 288 b., 289 a.
Artek oy ab 30, 31, 32 a., 33 a., 33 b.r., 34 a.
courtesy of Artifort 108, 110-113, 115
courtesy B&B Italia 130, 134 a., 135, 158-162, 166-167, 196-199, 200 b., 245, 250-251, 253, 254-255, 26 a., 280
© BD BARCELONA DESIGN 272 b., 273
Henrich von der Becke 61
Belux AG 258
Ronan & Erwan Bouroullec 312 b.l., 313 a.r., 313 b., 314 a.r.
Caimi Brevetti S.p.A. 2011 133
courtesy of Estudio Campana 174 b., 175, 176 b., 178 a.l.
courtesy of Cappellini 235, 236, 238, 239 b., 266, 284 b., 314 b.
courtesy of Carl Hansen & Son A/S 82, 84-85, 86 a., 89 a.
Maro Carrieri, property of Knoll Archive 80b.
Cassina I Contemporanei Collection 138 b., 140, 141, 188, 190, 191, 206-207, 209, 214, 284 a.
Cassina I Contemporanei Collection, Ruy Teixeira 132 b.
Cassina I Maestri Collection
p. 20 LC-1: Le Corbusier, Pierre Jeanneret, Charlotte Perriand
p. 22 LC-2: Le Corbusier, Pierre Jeanneret, Charlotte Perriand
p. 22 LC-10-P: Le Corbusier, Pierre Jeanneret, Charlotte Perriand
p. 23 LC-4: Le Corbusier, Pierre Jeanneret, Charlotte Perriand
p. 24/25 LC-3: Le Corbusier, Pierre Jeanneret, Charlotte Perriand
p. 24/25 LC-14: Le Corbusier
p. 26 LC-7: Le Corbusier, Pierre Jeanneret, Charlotte Perriand
p. 26 LC-8: Le Corbusier, Pierre Jeanneret, Charlotte Perriand
p. 27 LC-15: Le Corbusier
p. 28 Tokyo Chaise-Longue: Charlotte Perriand
p. 29 Ombra: Charlotte Perriand

courtesy Studio Museo Achille Castiglioni 95
Federico Cedrone, © Minotti S.p.A. 183
courtesy of ClassiCon 8-13, 270-271, 275
Collection georges pompidou Dist. RMN / Georges Mergueditchian 46 b.
Marco Covi, Triest 148, 150, 152, 154, 156-157
Michael Cullen, property of Knoll Archive 81 a., 81 b.l., 90
Paul Denton 169
Courtesy and © 2011 Eames Office, LLC (eamesoffice.com) 69, 70 a. (sketch)
courtesy of edra 174, 176 a., 177-181
Robert Fischer 303, 319
courtesy of Fiskars/Iittala 35 a.
© FLC 21
Fritz Hansen A/S 50-59, 86 b., 116-123
Beate Gerber 60, 62 a., 63, 67
courtesy Glas Italia 212
Katharina Gossow 263
Peter Guenzel, courtesy of Established & Sons 241 a., 276 a.b. 322 b.
Rainer Hosch, courtesy of MDF ITALIA 279
© interlübke 262, 264
Ditte Isager 203
© Jäger & Jäger 226, 228-231
© Markus Jans 227
Anna Kiuru 33 b.l.
Courtesy of Knoll Archive 17 a., 18 b., 19 b, b r., 81 ., 92 a., b r., 9 3a.
Nikola Koenig, property of Knoll Archive 18 a.
Ingmar Kurth, courtesy of e15 320 a., b.r., 321 b.l., 322 a., 323 a.r., b.l.
courtesy of Richard Lampert 64-66
Jouko Lehtola 201 a.
courtesy Lema and Santi Caleca 211
Bart Van Leuven / OWI 217
Ligne Roset 114
Kaj Lindqvist, JMG Studio 34 b.
courtesy of Living Divani 202, 204-205, 208, 213, 215
Pedro Llorca, courtesy of Viccarbe 281 a.
David Lundberg 35 b.
courtesy of Magis S.p.A. 137, 192, 194-195, 233, 234 b., 237 a., 267 a., 269, 277 a., 277 m. 312 a.r., 313 a.
courtesy of matteograssi 300
MatzForm 107
Joshua McHugh, property of Knoll Archive 19a., 78, 93b.
courtesy of MDF ITALIA 225, 278, 285, 288
© Alberto Meda 145r., 145 b., 146 a., 324
© Minotti S.p.A. 182, 184-187, 189

© Nils Holger Moormann 228 b.r.
courtesy of Moroso 136, 138 a., 139, 168, 170, 171 b., 242, 243, 244, 246, 247, 258, 249, 252, 256b., 257, 268
Naoto Fukasawa Design 193
Rob Overmeer 259
© Verner Panton Design (Basel) 105
courtesy Pastoe 219 b.
courtesy of Plank Collezioni Srl 272 a.r., 274 b.
courtesy of Poliform 286, 287
courtesy of Poltrona Frau 97 b., 283, 289 m., 289 b.
courtesy of Porro Industria Mobili SRL 210, 265, 282
Richard Powers, property of Knoll Archive 16 a.
PP Møbler 83, 87, 88, 89 b.
© Dieter Rams 125
© Ola Rindal 311
courtesy of sdr+ 32 b., 124, 126-129
Mikkio Sekita, property of Knoll Archive 80 a., 92 b.
courtesy of Swedese Möbler 200 a.
Paul Tahon and Ronan & Erwan Bouroullec 316 m.
Thonet GmbH, Frankenberg 17 b., 36-39, 40-43, 201 b., 221, 223, 224, 324
Tom Vack, courtesy of Magis S.p.A. 310. 312 a.l., 313 b.
courtesy of Viccarbe 281 b.
courtesy of Walter Knoll AG & Co.KG 290, 291, 292-299, 301
Wilde+Spieth 62 b.
courtesy of Wilkhahn 325, 332
courtesy of Schönbuch GmbH 326, 327
Axel Struwe, courtesy of Böwer GmbH 267 b.
Martin Url 321 b.l., 321 a., b.r., 323 a.l., b.r.
© USM U. Schärer Söhne AG 100-103
© Vitra (www.vitra.com) 44, 46-49 (Jean Prouvé), 68, 70-77, 104, 106, 328 (Verner Panton), 142, 144-145, 146 m. (Alberto Meda), 163-165 (Antonio Citterio), 171 a. (Ron Arad), 216, 218, 219 a. (Maarten van Severen), 232, 234 a., 237 b., 239 a., 240 a. (Jasper Morrison), 260-261 (Hella Jongerius), 266 b. (Werner Aisslinger), 277 b. (Konstantin Grcic), 312, b.r., 313 a.l., 313 m., 314 a.l., 316 a., 316 b., 317 (Ronan & Erwan Bouroullec)
Zanotta Spa - Italy 94, 96, 97 a., 98, 99